Eyes Open 3
Student's Book — Combo B

Ben Goldstein & **Ceri Jones**
with **Eoin Higgins**

Unit	Vocabulary	Reading	Language focus 1	Listening and vocabulary
5 **Let's talk**	p53 Communication	p54 A survey **Explore** communication collocations	p55 *will, might/may* + adverbs of possibility ▶ Social networks	p56 Short conversations Communication verbs
6 **Fears**	p63 Fears	p64 An advice column **Explore** prepositional phrases **Get it right!** *advice*	p65 *be going to/will*/Present continuous ▶ Creepy creatures	p66 Conversations between friends *-ed* and *-ing* adjectives **Get it right!** *bored/boring*
	Review Unit 5 and 6 page 72–73			
7 **School life**	p75 Life at school	p76 A student blog **Explore** words in context **Get it right!** *want* + infinitive	p77 Second conditional ▶ The women of Ayoquesco p97 **Say it right!** Intonation in second conditional sentences	p78 A discussion *make* and *do*
8 **Green planet**	p85 Materials **Get it right!** *the* and plural nouns p97 **Say it right!** Stress in compound words	p86 An article **Explore** words in context	p87 Present simple passive **Get it right!** active vs. passive ▶ Where does it all go?	p88 A class presentation Energy issues
	Review Unit 7 and 8 page 94–95			

Projects p125   Irregular verbs and phonemic script: back of book

Language focus 2	Discover Culture (Video and Reading)	Speaking	Writing	Extras
p57 First conditional + *may/might*, *be able to* **Get it right!** *if* clauses **p97 Say it right!** Intonation in first conditional sentences	**p58** ⏵ The language of the future? **p59** An article **Explore** phrasal verbs	**p60** ⏵ **Real talk:** Have you ever given a class presentation? Reassuring someone	**p61** An essay **Useful language:** Introducing points and arguments	**p119 CLIL** Technology – Early written communication ⏵ Pictures with meaning **p103 Grammar reference** **p111 Vocabulary bank**
p67 Quantifiers *a little/a few* **p97 Say it right!** *ough*	**p68** ⏵ Calendar of the ancient Maya **p69** An article **Explore** opposites	**p70** ⏵ **Real talk:** What are you afraid of? Expressing surprise	**p71** An email to a friend **Useful language:** Introducing news and explaining things	**p120 CLIL** Geography – Living in a global city ⏵ City or country? **p104 Grammar reference** **p112 Vocabulary bank**
p79 Second conditional questions	**p80** ⏵ Playing with Maths **p81** An article **Explore** phrasal verbs	**p82** ⏵ **Real talk:** Who would you talk to if you needed advice? Asking for and giving advice	**p83** A problem page **Useful language:** Summarising a problem and giving advice	**p121 CLIL** Technology – Social media ⏵ Be safe online **p105 Grammar reference** **p113 Vocabulary bank**
p89 Past simple passive Past simple passive question forms	**p90** ⏵ Build it better **p91** An article **Explore** phrasal verbs	**p92** ⏵ **Real talk:** What kind of voluntary work can you do in your school or town? Apologising and explaining	**p93** A newspaper article **Useful language:** Using direct speech	**p122 CLIL** Chemistry – Renewable energy ⏵ Driving into the future **p106 Grammar reference** **p114 Vocabulary bank**

5 Let's talk

In this unit ...

Social networks **p55**

The language of the future? **p58**

Giving a presentation **p60**

CLIL Pictures with meaning **p119**

Vocabulary
- Communication
- Communication collocations
- Communication verbs
- Phrasal verbs

Language focus
- *will*, *might/may* + adverbs of possibility and probability: *definitely*, *probably*
- First conditional

Unit aims
I can ...
- describe different ways of communicating.
- talk about events that I'm sure and not sure about in the future.
- talk about possible situations in the future.
- understand about English as a world language.
- reassure someone.
- write an essay about the best way to communicate.

BE CURIOUS

What can you see in the photo?
Start thinking
- What are the children doing?
- Are they communicating with each other?
- What do you think about how they are communicating?

Vocabulary
Communication

1 🔊 **2.01** Match the words in the box with the pictures (a–f). Which pictures are missing? Then listen, check and repeat.

> Tweet   text message   social media post
> email   ~~chatting~~   phone call   Skype™
> forum   blog post

a *chatting*

2 Match the missing pictures from Exercise 1 to the definitions.
1. A message of 140 characters.
2. When you write information about yourself to share with others.
3. An online diary.

3 Match the comments with a form of communication from the box in Exercise 1.
1. Hi, this is Susan. Sorry, I can't talk at the moment. Please leave me a message after the beep! *phone call*
2. Please find attached the form. You need to complete it and send it back to me.
3. Hi Grandma, can you see me OK? I can hear you but there's no video. Can you turn your webcam on?
4. @RM_Players celebrate in the street. We won the league again! #victory
5. OK Tanya, CU on Fri at 7:30 @ the cinema. Txt me if u get lost!
6. Barbara has added 17 new photos to her album Life in Leeds.

4 🔊 **2.02** Listen to the conversation. What forms of communication do they talk about from Exercise 1?

Your turn

5 Put the forms of communication from Exercise 1 in order of when you most often use them.

6 Work with a partner. Compare your answers from Exercise 5. Then complete the quiz and compare your answers.

> I've got text messages first because I send hundreds of texts every day!

1 How often do you use these forms of communication?

	several times a day	once a day	once a week	less
phone				
email				
text				
Tweet				
Skype™				

2 What do you usually post on social media, Twitter or blogs?

☐ my life   ☐ school   ☐ news
☐ jokes   ☐ photos
☐ other (please specify) ....

➡ **Vocabulary Bank** • page 111

Reading A survey

1 Work with a partner. Look at the photo. Is the situation familiar to you?

2 🔊 **2.03** Read the introduction to an online survey. What is it about?
a face-to-face communication
b teenagers and communication
c teenagers and computers

3 🔊 **2.04** Read the survey. Then work with a partner, answer the questions and read the results.

HOW DO YOU COMMUNICATE?

A recent survey showed that although 80% of UK teens have more than 400 Facebook friends, they have only met a quarter of these friends in real life. Psychologists worry that teens in the future might lose the ability to make friends face-to-face and will only communicate through Tweets, online forums and status updates. Is that true for you? Complete our social networking survey and find out!

1 WHAT'S THE BEST WAY TO MAKE FRIENDS?
A Social networking sites like Facebook and Twitter.
B It depends on the person.
C Face-to-face.

2 HOW WILL SOCIAL NETWORKS CHANGE IN THE NEXT TEN YEARS?
A They will get more popular.
B There will probably be a lot more of them.
C They definitely won't disappear but people might get bored with them and go back to chatting over a coffee.

3 IS THERE A DANGER OF HAVING TOO MANY ONLINE FRIENDS?
A No, it's how the digital generation meet.
B It depends on how many real-life friends you have.
C Yes, people might forget how to communicate in real life.

4 WHICH SENTENCE MIGHT BE TRUE FOR YOU IN FIVE YEARS' TIME?
A You'll certainly have a lot more online friends.
B You'll have the same number of friends both online and in real life.
C You may need to start making friends online.

Explore communication collocations

4 Match the words and phrases from the survey with the definitions below.

> status update   face-to-face   virtual friends
> digital generation   social network sites

1 a post about your current activity, thoughts or feelings
2 group of people who have grown up with digital technology
3 people you can see and speak to on a computer
4 directly, meeting in the same place
5 a website that helps people communicate and share information

➔ **Vocabulary Bank** • page 111

Your turn

5 Discuss the following statements. Do you agree or disagree?
Most of my friends …
a communicate through their status updates every day.
b access social networks by phone or tablet.
c have met their virtual friends (on social media, Twitter etc.) in real life.
d don't have a social network account but they would like to have one.

RESULTS

Mostly A: You love social media (but you may love it too much). You're great at making virtual friends. But what about real life? Do you have enough friends there too?

Mostly B: You like to use a bit of both. You have a good mixture of online and real-life friends.

Mostly C: You prefer face-to-face communication but you also know you might need to use social networks for your job or studies one day.

FACT! *Facebook has over 1 billion active users. 30% of them are in Europe.*

Language focus 1 *will, might/may* + adverbs of possibility

1 Look at the examples from the text on page 54. Write (C) certain or (NC) not certain. Then complete the rules.

a They **will get** more popular. *C*
b You **may need** to start making friends online.
c There **will probably be** a lot more of them.
d They **definitely won't** disappear.
e You'll **certainly have** a lot more online friends.
f They **might not** disappear.

We use ¹.... and ².... to show we are sure about the future. We use ³..../.... to show we are not sure about the future. We use *probably*, *definitely* and *certainly* to show how sure we are.

Grammar reference • page 103

2 Complete the sentences. Use the verbs and prompts in brackets to help you.

1 I'm sure everyone ....*will have*.... an Internet connection in the future. (*have* – certain)
2 I .... my mobile phone next month, I'm not sure yet. (*change* – not certain)
3 My brother .... ever .... all his friends on social media, it's impossible, he's got too many! (*meet* – certain)
4 I don't know, I .... tonight – I have a lot of work to do. (*go online* – not certain)
5 My grandparents .... definitely .... me later, it's cheaper than a phone call. (*Skype™* – certain)
6 Our teacher .... us next week, so you should listen. (*test* – not certain)

3 Use the prompts to write sentences using your own ideas. Use the adverbs *definitely, probably* and *certainly* in the correct position.

1 social networks / with us / for a long time. *Social networks will definitely be with us for a long time.*
2 lose contact / friends you have now
3 make / new friends in the future
4 tablets / more popular than smartphones in the future
5 online friends / not replace real-life friends in my lifetime

4 🔊 2.05 Complete the blog post with the words in the box. Then listen, check and repeat.

will (x3)   won't   probably   might (x3)

A techno geek speaks out:

In the near future, machines ¹....*will*.... do everything for us. There ².... be any books, only screens. We ³.... won't need teachers, because we ⁴.... definitely be able to learn everything on our own. I imagine that some of you ⁵.... not like the idea because you're frightened of change, but it's good! As for communication, who knows, we ⁶.... see the end of telephones. I'm not sure but I think television ⁷.... disappear too – we ⁸.... probably watch everything on our computers!

Your turn

5 Make predictions about your lives. Use *will, might/may* and adverbs of probability. Write five sentences.

My family will probably visit a foreign country in the future.
Our teacher will definitely give us homework tonight.

6 Work with a partner. Compare and discuss your ideas.

Learn about communicating online.
• What social network sites do you use?
• Which three social networks do they talk about in the video?
• Why are they 'changing the Internet'?

5.1 Social networks

Vocabulary
Communication verbs

1 🔊 **2.06** Complete the sentences with the correct form of the words in the box. Then listen and check.

> whisper   complain   boast   gossip   ~~argue~~
> joke   shout   criticise

1 Don't ..**argue**.. with me – you know that I'm right!
2 You shouldn't .... about the bad weather – what do you expect in England in November!
3 I don't like him. He's always .... about people behind their backs.
4 It's true that she does well at school, but she doesn't need to .... about it.
5 You shouldn't .... with your friends about something serious. They might not think it's funny.
6 Emmet is my friend, so don't .... him. And anyway, nobody's perfect!
7 Sshh! I'm trying to study. If you want to talk, please .... !
8 Those boys are always ..... . They're so noisy!!

Your turn

2 Make notes about three of the situations.
1 a time when you argued with someone
2 the last time you complained about something
3 the last time someone criticised you
4 a time when someone shouted at you
5 someone you know who boasts a lot
6 a time when you joked with someone and they didn't think it was funny

I argued with my brother last week. It was about the computer.

My teacher criticised me yesterday because I forgot my homework again.

3 Ask and answer with your partner about your situations. Find out more information.
A: When was the last time you argued with someone?
B: I argued with my sister about the computer.
A: Why did you argue about the computer?

➡ **Vocabulary Bank** • page 111

Listening Short conversations

4 Work with a partner. Look at the photos of four different conversations and answer the questions.
1 Where are the people?
2 What is the relationship between them?
3 What do you think they are talking about?

a

b

c

d

5 🔊 **2.07** Listen to four short conversations. Match the photos in Exercise 4 to the conversations.

6 🔊 **2.07** Listen again. Answer the questions.
Conversation 1
1 What is Serena's problem?
2 What does her mother promise?
Conversation 2
1 What does Alex want Nick to do?
2 What's Alex's opinion of football?
Conversation 3
1 What does Bella say about Rachel?
2 What is Tina's reaction?
Conversation 4
1 When does the concert start?
2 How does Paul make his friend hurry up?

Language focus 2 First Conditional + *may/might, be able to*

1 Complete the examples from the listening on page 56.
1. If you *pass* all your exams, we *'ll have* a holiday abroad this year.
2. We …. in the cup final **if** we **win** tonight.
3. If you **wear** make-up, they …. **send** you home.
4. If you …. first in the queue, you**'ll get** to meet the band!
5. You …. the band if you**'re** late.

2 Look at the examples again. Use the words in the box to change or add more information.

> definitely send   may have   be able to
> probably meet   might miss

1. If you pass all your exams, we …. a holiday abroad this year.
2. We'll …. be in the cup final if we win tonight.
3. If you wear make-up to school, they'll …. you home.
4. If you're first in the queue you'll …. the band.
5. You …. the band if you're late.

3 Look at the examples in Exercises 1 and 2 and choose the words to complete the rules.

> 1. We use the first conditional to talk about possible situations in the *past / future*.
> 2. We can use *might/may*, and *be able to* instead of *will / the present simple*.
> 3. When we use adverbs they come *before / after* the verb.

 Grammar reference • page 103

Get it right!
When the *if* clause comes first, it ends with a comma (,).
If we meet the band, I'll be really happy.

4 Use the prompts to write sentences.
1. you whisper / not be able to hear you
   If you whisper, she won't be able to hear you.
2. if / you post an update / I definitely / read it
3. I / text you / if / get lost
4. if / she speak quickly / I might not / understand
5. you / might make / new friends / if / join the club
6. if / they practise a lot / be able to win

5 Complete the text with the correct form of the verbs in brackets.

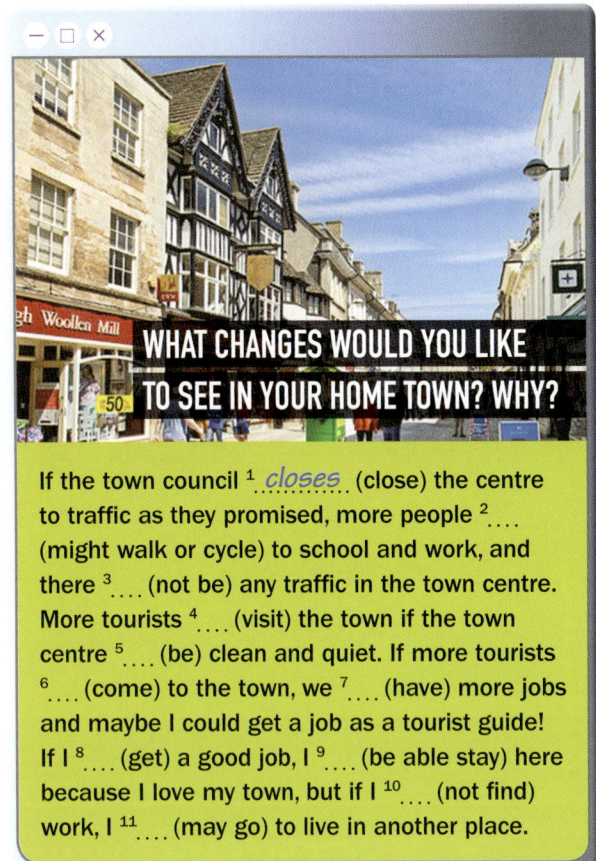

WHAT CHANGES WOULD YOU LIKE TO SEE IN YOUR HOME TOWN? WHY?

If the town council ^{1} *closes* (close) the centre to traffic as they promised, more people ^{2} …. (might walk or cycle) to school and work, and there ^{3} …. (not be) any traffic in the town centre. More tourists ^{4} …. (visit) the town if the town centre ^{5} …. (be) clean and quiet. If more tourists ^{6} …. (come) to the town, we ^{7} …. (have) more jobs and maybe I could get a job as a tourist guide! If I ^{8} …. (get) a good job, I ^{9} …. (be able stay) here because I love my town, but if I ^{10} …. (not find) work, I ^{11} …. (may go) to live in another place.

Say it right! • page 96

Your turn

6 Complete three of the sentences below so that they are true for you. Then write two more sentences.

If the weather is good over the weekend, …
If I don't pass all my exams, …
If I have enough money, …
If I argue with my parents.
If I criticise my friend.
If I shout at my teacher.

If the weather is good over the weekend, I'll go out with my friends for a picnic. If we go out for a picnic, we'll probably take a guitar with us. If we take a guitar, I'll definitely sing some songs.

7 Work with a partner. Compare your sentences.

Discover Culture

1. Look at the photos. They refer to the two topics in the video about China. Think about the questions below.
   1. What does China produce? Do you have any items produced in China with you now?
   2. What languages do Chinese people speak?

Find out about Mandarin.

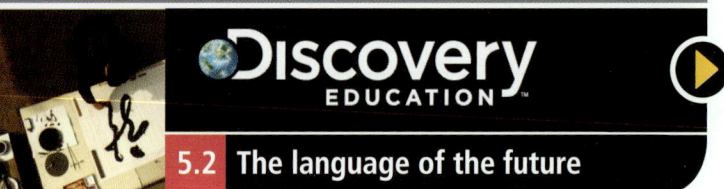

5.2 The language of the future

2. ▶ 5.2 Watch the video and check your answers.

3. ▶ 5.2 Watch the video again. What do you hear about these numbers?
   1. 1.4 billion   3. 1950s
   2. 40,000   4. 10 or 20 years

4. Watch the video again. Choose the correct answer.
   1. China's population is bigger than
      a. Europe's.   b. the United States'.
      c. Europe and the United States' together.
   2. The Chinese people speak
      a. different languages.   b. Mandarin.   c. English.
   3. In written Mandarin, people use
      a. 40,000 characters.   b. three or four thousand characters.
      c. four thousand characters.
   4. The Pinyin system uses
      a. the Roman alphabet.   b. Chinese characters.   c. a computer.
   5. More people speak .... in the world than English.
      a. Mandarin   b. Roman   c. French

5. Test your memory. What did you see when you heard these phrases?
   1. Everything in China is growing.
   2. The country produces so many things.
   3. Every day, more and more people use Mandarin to communicate.

6. ▶ 5.2 Watch the video again and check your answers.

Your turn

7. Discuss the questions in groups.
   1. What does your country produce? Does it go to many other countries?
   2. Would you like to learn Mandarin? Why/Why not? Why would it be useful?
   3. Is your language a difficult language to learn for foreign learners? Why?/Why not?

Reading An article

1 Work with a partner. Look at the pictures and answer the questions.
1 Where would you see the images?
2 Why do you think they are in English?

2 🔊 **2.10** Read the article about the English language. Is English still the world's number one language?

3 Read the article again. Mark the sentences true (T) or false (F). Correct the false ones.
1 English is everywhere because a lot of people understand it.
2 There are fewer second language speakers of English than native speakers.
3 In Denmark, people speak English as a second language.
4 The English language has the most words.
5 *Selfie* and *app* are old words.
6 The author is sure that Mandarin will be the world's next number one language.

Explore phrasal verbs

4 Look at the highlighted words in the text. Match the phrasal verbs in the box to the definitions.

> go up   get by   keep on   come into use   turn into

1 When a figure or number increases or gets bigger.
2 Start being used.
3 When something changes and becomes something different.
4 To be able to live with a situation with difficulty.
5 When you continue to do something.

➡ **Vocabulary Bank** • page 111

Your turn

5 Complete the sentences about English with your own ideas. Then compare your sentences.
1 I enjoy/don't enjoy learning English because …
2 Learning English is difficult because …
3 I sometimes use English …
4 I think in the future I will use English …

I enjoy learning because I like talking to …

THE WORLD OF ENGLISH

Almost everywhere you go in the world, you'll see English. It's on signs, adverts and T-shirts! In the online world, it's even more obvious. Why? Because it is the one language that most people understand – more than Mandarin or Spanish, which have more native speakers than English.

So, how many people speak English? Right now there are over 360 million native speakers of English in the world. And a similar number of people speak it as a second language. But there are more than a billion people who speak or are learning English and that figure is **going up**. In countries like Denmark, Singapore or Israel more than 80% of people speak English. So, if you go there, you'll find it easy to **get by**!

There are also more words in English than in almost any other language. At the moment, there are over a million words in English and we **keep on** adding more words. You might know words like *selfie*, *Tweet*, *app* and *chillax*. All of these words have **come into use** in the English language in the last few years.

And what about the future? Will English always be the world's number one language? For the moment, yes, but if the Chinese economy continues to grow, will Mandarin **turn into** the next number one world language? We'll have to wait and see!

FACT! *Soon there will be more people in China who speak English as a foreign language than there are native English speakers in the whole world!*

Speaking Reassuring someone

Real talk: Have you ever given a class presentation?

1 ▶ 5.3 Watch the teenagers in the video. How many teenagers …
a) have given a class presentation?
b) are nervous or worried about giving class presentations?
c) have to do class presentations regularly?

2 💬 Have *you* ever given a class presentation?

3 🔊 2.11 Helen is talking to her older sister Petra. What is Helen worried about?

4 Complete the conversation with the useful language.

Useful language

Don't worry!
You don't need to worry.
You'll be fine (I'm sure).
Listen, I think I can help you.

It'll turn out all right.
There's no problem!
Of course you can (do it)!

5 🔊 2.11 Listen again and check your answers.

6 💬 Work with a partner. Practise the conversation in Exercise 4.

7 💬 Change the words in bold in the conversation. Use the ideas below. Take turns to ask and answer the questions.

Problem 1
You have to sing a song at the talent competition.

Problem 2
You are playing in the final of a tennis competition.

Petra: What's the matter Helen? You look worried.
Helen: I've got to **give a presentation in English class next week**, and I'm scared. I don't think I can do it!
Petra: Of ¹ *course* you can! You're good at English. You ² …. to worry.
Helen: Yes, but you know I'm really **shy**. It's frightening in front of all those people!
Petra: True, it's not easy if you're **shy**, but don't ³…. ! You'll ⁴…. , I'm sure.
Helen: Well, the problem is, when I **speak in class I feel embarrassed and go red**. Then I **mix up the words**.
Petra: Hmm! Listen, I think I can ⁵…. . Have you **written the presentation** yet?
Helen: Well, yes, I've **more or less finished it**.
Petra: Then ⁶…. no problem! You can practise it **on me and my friends**.
Helen: OK! That sounds like a good idea. I'll feel more confident then.
Petra: Yes. If you practise it lots of times, I know it'll turn out ⁷…. .

Writing An essay

1 Look at the photo and read the essay. Choose the best title.
  a Have mobile phones improved communication for teenagers?
  b Are teenagers too dependent on mobile phones?

Twenty years ago, mobile phones were for business people. Nowadays, it's impossible to find a teenager without one, but are mobiles the best way for teenagers to communicate? Mobiles can be useful. Firstly, they allow teenagers to communicate with their friends and family anywhere, anytime. Sending text messages is also quick and cheap. What's more, mobiles help you organise your life, and you can tell your parents what you're doing so they don't worry.

However, there are negatives. For one thing, you might not have a signal, especially in the countryside. In addition, if you are in a noisy place, you can't hear your mobile ring. Lastly, using it all the time can be expensive.

On balance, I think mobiles have definitely improved communication for teenagers. Nevertheless, they mustn't use them too much.

2 Read the essay again. Answer the questions.
  1 How does the writer get the reader's attention in the introduction?
  2 How many arguments in favour of mobile phones are there?
  3 How many arguments against mobile phones are there?
  4 What is his/her opinion of mobile phones for teenagers?

Useful language

Introducing points and arguments
Use adverbs and other phrases to introduce what you want to say.
Nowadays, …   What's more, …   Nevertheless,
Firstly, …   However, …

3 Look at the Useful language box. Find four other words or phrases to introduce arguments in the essay.

4 Complete the sentences with the words in the box.

  addition   lastly   more   ~~one thing~~   Firstly

  1 I recommend this mobile. For *one thing*, it's a smartphone. What's …, it's on special offer, and …, it's quite small and light.
  2 The new model has two improvements. …, it has a much bigger memory, and in …, the battery will last longer.

PLAN

5 Plan an essay. Include information from Exercise 4 to help you and the plan below.
Title: Are social networking sites like Facebook the best way for teenagers to communicate?
  • an introduction
  • a paragraph with arguments in favour
  • a paragraph with arguments against
  • a conclusion, including your opinion

WRITE

6 Write your essay. Use your notes from Exercise 5 and the model text to help you.

CHECK

7 Can you say YES to these questions?
  • Is the information from the plan in your essay?
  • Have you used expressions like *Firstly, What's more,* etc. in your essay?

6 Fears

Discovery EDUCATION

In this unit …

Creepy creatures **p65**

Calendars of the ancient Maya **p68**

What are you afraid of? **p70**

CLIL City or country **p120**

Vocabulary
- Fears
- Prepositional phrases
- ending in -ed and -ing
- Opposites

Language focus
- going to/will/Present continuous
- Quantifiers

Unit aims
I can …
- talk about fears.
- talk about things I will and won't do in the future.
- talk about how I feel.
- understand about superstitions.
- express surprise and disbelief.
- write an email to a friend about plans and problems.

BE CURIOUS

Look at the photo on this page.
What can you see in the photo?
Start thinking
- Where are the people?
- Why are they there?
- What isn't the man afraid of?

Vocabulary Fears

1 🔊 **2.12** Match the words in the box with the photos of fears (a–g). Which word is not in the photos? Then listen, check and repeat.

> flying   heights   ~~the dark~~   lifts   insects   birds   clowns   snakes

a *the dark*

2 🔊 **2.13** Listen and match the speakers to the fears in Exercise 1.

1 *birds*

Your turn

3 How afraid are you of the things in Exercise 1? Put them in order. Add one or two of your own fears to the list.

1 *heights*   2 *snakes*

4 Ask and answer with your partner. Compare your list.
1 Do you know anyone who has any of these fears or other common ones?
2 How does the fear change his/her behaviour?

My mum has a fear of flying. She drives really long distances to avoid going on a plane!

➡ **Vocabulary Bank** • page 112

Reading An advice column

1 Look at the photos. What do you think the teenagers are afraid of?

2  2.14 Read the online advice column and check your answer.

3 Read the advice column again. Answer the questions.
  1. What is the difference between a fear and a phobia?
  2. Why does Isabella have to travel?
  3. What is Mary's advice to Isabella?
  4. Why does Kevin have to travel?
  5. What is Kevin worried about?
  6. What is Mary's advice to Kevin?

Explore prepositional phrases

4 Look at the highlighted phrases in the text. Complete the sentences with the correct prepositions after the verbs or adjectives.
  1. My mother's terrified .... flying.
  2. I'm very worried .... going up in the lift.
  3. What do you think .... my new dress? Do you like it?
  4. Are you going to share that chocolate .... me?
  5. I'm a bit embarrassed .... my fear of insects.

→ **Vocabulary Bank** • page 112

> **Get it right!**
> *Advice* doesn't have a plural form and cannot be used with *a* or *an*.
> Maria gave good **advice**. ✓
> ~~Maria gave good advices.~~ ✗
> ~~Maria gave a good advice.~~ ✗

Your turn

5 Ask and answer with your partner.
  1. Do you know of any other famous people who have fears or phobias? What are their fears?
  2. Do you think Mary gave good advice? Do you think it's easy to help people with phobias? Why?/Why not?

Yes, I think … is afraid of …
Yes, I think it's very/quite good because she …
No, I don't think it's very good because …
I think it's easy/difficult to help people with phobias because …

ASK MARY

Today we're going to look at fears and phobias. Everybody's afraid of something and famous people have fears, too. Did you know that Daniel Radcliffe is scared of clowns and Scarlett Johansson has a phobia of birds? For most people, these fears aren't very important. However, when a fear becomes a phobia – a strong fear you can't control – it can cause serious problems.

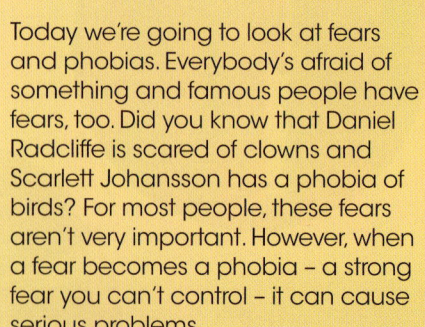
ISABELLA, 13 (FLORIDA)

'My uncle's getting married next month and my parents and I are going to the wedding – in San Francisco! I'm **terrified of** flying and the flight takes four and a half hours. What am I going to do?'

Lots of people are afraid of flying. Jennifer Aniston, for example, hates planes, so you're in good company! Try to get some exercise before the flight so you'll feel tired and then you'll probably sleep on the plane. Listen to your favourite music. When you feel nervous, close your eyes and take long, deep breaths and you'll be fine!

KEVIN, 14 (LIVERPOOL)

'I can't sleep at night without a light. Next week, I'm travelling to London on a school trip and I'm going to **share a room with** other students. They'll definitely want to switch off the lights and I won't be able to sleep. I don't want them to think I'm a baby! Please help. I'm really **worried about** it!'

Don't be **embarrassed about** it. Did you know that Keanu Reeves is afraid of the dark? And no one says he's a baby! Don't worry about what other people will **think of** you. Just tell your roommates that you want a light on at night like it's the most normal thing in the world. They probably won't say anything about it.

FACT! Arachnophobia, the fear of spiders, is the most common phobia. Millions of people around the world suffer from it.

Language focus 1 *be going to/will/Present continuous*

1 Match the sentences from the text on page 64 with the uses (a–c).
1 I'm **going** to share a room with other students.
2 They probably **won't** say anything about it.
3 My uncle**'s getting** married next month.
a a definite arrangement
b a personal intention
c a prediction

➡ **Grammar reference** • page 104

2 Join the parts of the sentences.
1 We aren't going to
2 Don't watch that film
3 Are you going
4 Alice is flying to Spain
5 John's afraid of the dark so
6 I'm seeing our teacher

a to visit her aunty this summer.
b he'll probably sleep with the light on.
c take the lift.
d to watch a horror film this evening?
e at 4 pm about the school trip.
f or you'll have nightmares.

3 🔊 **2.15** Choose the correct option to complete the conversation. Then listen and check.

Your turn

4 Make notes about the questions below.
1 What job will you do when you're older?
2 When do you think you'll get married?
3 Will you still live in your town/village?
4 What are you doing after school today?
5 What are you going to do this weekend?
6 What are you going to do in the school holidays?

5 Ask and answer with your partner. Use your notes from Exercise 4 to help you.

> I think I'll be a doctor when I'm older.

> I think I'll be a teacher, but I'm not sure yet.

> This weekend, I'm going to watch a film with my friends.

Sally: ¹ Will you fly / **Are you flying** to San Francisco next week?
Isa: Yes, the taxi ² will arrive / is arriving at 7 am!
Sally: And when's the wedding?
Isa: It's on Thursday. We ³ are relaxing / 'll probably relax on Wednesday – ⁴ I'm going to go / I will go shopping with my cousin in the day. Then in the evening, my aunty has booked a restaurant and we ⁵ will eat / are eating together at 8 pm.
Sally: And after the wedding? ⁶ Will you / Are you going to stay in San Francisco for a holiday?
Isa: No, we ⁷ won't stay / aren't staying very long – our flight back ⁸ is leaving / will leave on Saturday morning.

Learn about a scary animal.
● What do you think is the scariest animal?
● What animal is the man trying to catch?
● How does the man catch it?

6.1 Creepy creatures

Listening Conversations between friends

1 Work with a partner. Look at the photo of the roller coaster and answer the questions.

1. How do you think the people on the roller coaster are feeling?
2. The ride is called *The Scream Machine*. Why do you think so?
3. Do you like roller coasters? Why/Why not?

2 🔊 2.16 Listen to two conversations between a group of friends in a theme park. How do Anita and Bruno feel a) at the beginning of the day and b) at the end of the day?

3 🔊 2.16 Listen again. Choose the correct answers.

Conversation 1
1. Which ride is Anita scared of?
   a The Scream Machine b The Colossus
   c The Tidal Wave
2. How does Bruno feel about The Tidal Wave?
   a He's terrified. b He's worried.
   c He's relaxed.
3. Why does Claudia suggest starting with The Scream Machine?
   a The queue is short. b It's very scary.
   c It's lots of fun.

Conversation 2
4. What was Claudia's favourite ride?
   a The Colossus b The Tidal Wave
   c The Scream Machine
5. What is the problem at the end of the day?
   a They miss the bus home.
   b They've spent a lot of money.
   c They can't get anything to eat.

Vocabulary *-ed* and *-ing* adjectives

4 🔊 2.17 Look at the pictures and example sentences. Circle the correct words. Then listen, check and repeat.

I'm terrified.

It's terrifying.

1. I'm really **bored** / boring. There's nothing to do!
2. The film we saw last night was **terrified / terrifying**!
3. Yesterday we looked at the physics of roller coasters in class. It was very **interested / interesting**.
4. We took my little cousins to a theme park at the weekend. They were really **excited / exciting**!
5. Yesterday we went on a 20-kilometre walk in the country. It was really **tired / tiring**!
6. I'm a bit **worried / worrying**. I have to give a presentation to the whole class tomorrow!

👁 Get it right!

I'm bored. = how we feel
It's boring. = something that causes that feeling
We use **in** with **interested** and **of** with **afraid/scared/frightened/terrified**.
I'm very interested in snakes.
Anita's terrified of roller coasters.

Your turn

5 Complete the sentences so that they're true for you.
1. I'm really interested in …
2. Today was really tiring because …
3. I'm excited about …
4. … is boring because …
5. I think … is/are terrifying because …
6. I'm worried about …

I'm really interested in fashion.

6 Work with a partner. Compare your sentences.
A: *I'm really interested in fashion.*
B: *I don't think fashion is very interesting. I'm really interested in music.*

➡ **Vocabulary Bank** • page 112

Language focus 2 Quantifiers

1 Complete the examples from the listening on page 66. Then complete the rules.

1 There are ..*too many*.. people. Look at the queue!
2 There's .... time to do everything. Don't worry about the queues.
3 How .... loops has it got?
4 We spent .... **much** money.
5 I'm hungry. **How** .... money have we got?

> 1 We use .... *much/many* to say an amount is excessive.
> 2 We use .... *much/many* to ask about quantity.
> 3 We use .... to say the amount is correct.

➡ **Grammar reference • page 104**

2 Choose the correct words.

1 There weren't **enough / much** rides.
2 We didn't go on everything. There were **too much / too many** rides.
3 **How much / How many** money did you spend at the park?
4 There weren't any shops and there weren't **many / much** restaurants either.
5 Did you have **enough / too many** time to go on all the rides?

a little / a few

3 Complete the examples from the listening on page 66. Then choose the word to complete the rule.

1 There are only .... people in the queue.
2 We've got .... time before the bus comes.

> We use *a little* and *a few* to express **big / small** quantities.

➡ **Grammar reference • page 104**

4 Complete the sentences using *a few* or *a little*.

1 We've got .... minutes before it opens.
2 There's .... pizza left. Do you want it?
3 Look! I took .... photos at the park.
4 I've only got .... pocket money.
5 We met .... friends at the park.

5 🔊 **2.18** Complete the conversation with the words in the box. Then listen and check.

> too much   a few   how many   enough
> a little   how much (x2)   too many   ~~not much~~

A: Let's go on the roller coaster again.
B: I don't think so. There's ¹ ..*not much*.. time before the bus comes.
A: But it's so amazing!
B: ² .... times do you want to go on it?
A: Well, OK, have we got ³ .... money to get a hot dog?
B: ⁴ .... are they?
A: They're £2 each.
B: Let's see. Yes, and we've got ⁵ .... extra money for something else!
A: Let's buy some more ice cream.
B: More? ⁶ .... ice cream can you eat?
A: I can never eat ⁷ .... ice cream!
B: I'm so tired. Let's sit down here for ⁸ .... minutes. I hope there aren't ⁹ .... people on the bus – I don't want to stand all the way home.

➡ **Say it right! • page 97**

Your turn

6 Makes notes about the questions below.

1 Have you ever been to a theme park? Did you like it?
2 Were there a lot of rides? Did you have enough time to go on all of them?
3 Were there a lot of people?
4 What rides were you afraid of at the park?

7 Ask and answer with your partner about a theme park. Use your notes in Exercise 6 to help you.

I went to a theme park called … last summer. It was great.

Discover Culture

1. **Work with a partner. Look at the photos and answer the questions.**
   1. In which country is this ancient city?
   2. Who lived there?
   3. What is the chart do you think?
   4. What is the connection with the sun and the moon?

Find out about the ancient Mayan calendar.

6.2 Calendars of the ancient Maya

2. 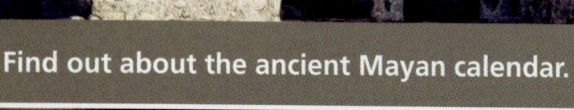 **6.2 Watch the first part of the video (to 1.14) and check your answers.**

3.  **6.2 Watch the first part of the video again and answer the questions.**
   1. What question did the Maya think they could answer?
   2. Why do scientists study the Mayan calendar?

4. 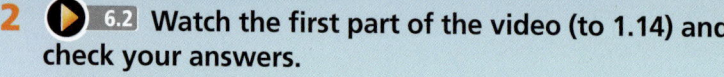 **6.2 Watch the next part of the video and complete the text.**

The calendar had 18 [1] .... of 20 days each, a total of [2] .... days.
Then there were five [3] .... days, a total of [4] .... days.
The calendar was very important. There are 365 [5] .... in the Kukulcan Temple: one for each day of the solar [6] ....

5. **Test your visual memory. Put these images in the correct order.**
   a. The Imix and Cimi symbols.
   b. The sun setting over a river.
   c. The moon passing above a palace.
   d. A view of a Mayan temple and beach.

6. **What do you remember about the calendar? Choose the correct word.**
   Imix was a [1] **good / bad** day. They planned to do [2] **enjoyable / important** things, like planting on these days. Cimi was a [3] **good / bad** day. Its symbol was the [4] **closed / open** eye of a dead person. [5] **Everything / Nothing** important happened on these days.

7. **6.2 Watch the whole video again and check your answers to Exercises 5 and 6.**

Your turn

8. **Work with a partner. Answer the questions.**
   1. Do you think it's possible to predict good days and bad days? Why?/ Why not?
   2. What's a good day for you? What's a bad day? Why? What kinds of things happen?

   A: *I think it's impossible, you never know what's going to happen.*
   B: *I think the weather's important – if it's sunny, it could be a good day.*

Superstitions? Who needs them!

Superstitions have been around for thousands of years. A lot of people never walk under ladders or they believe that black cats bring **good** (or bad) luck. Some people think one magpie is bad luck but two together is good luck. Other superstitions are more modern, like football players who don't change their socks or who always enter the pitch with their right foot.

Lots of people, however, believe strongly that superstitions are **silly**. They say that superstitions are based on **old** habits, customs or beliefs. How could you have bad luck by opening an umbrella inside? Why is the number thirteen more **dangerous** than other numbers?

To prove their point, they have 'Anti-Superstition Parties', usually on Friday the thirteenth, a date that many people think brings bad luck. At these parties, people break mirrors and dance with open umbrellas. And nothing bad happens!

Peter Moore, a dentist, has been to several anti-superstition parties. He says, 'People must be crazy to believe that the number seven is **lucky** or that they could be more **successful** by putting a horseshoe outside their house.' Chelsea Evans, a chef, agrees. 'I love the parties. I've broken lots of mirrors and my life is going well!'

FACT! Fear of the number 13 is called Triskaidekaphobia and fear of Friday the Thirteenth is called Friggatriskaidekaphobia.

Reading An article

1 Work with a partner. Look at the photos showing superstitions. What do you think the superstitions are?

2  Read the article and check your answers.
Have you got the same superstitions in your country?

3 Read the article again. Are the sentences true or false? Correct the false ones.
   1 All superstitions have a modern origin. *F*
   2 Some superstitions come from modern beliefs.
   3 Some football players wear two socks on one foot.
   4 Anti-superstition parties are for people who believe in superstitions.
   5 At anti-superstition parties, people don't follow any superstitions.
   6 Peter and Chelsea are scared to go to anti-superstition parties.

Explore opposite adjectives

4 Look at the highlighted adjectives in the text. Match them to the opposite adjectives below.
   1 safe   4 unlucky
   2 unsuccessful   5 bad
   3 modern   6 sensible

 Vocabulary Bank • page 112

Your turn

5 Write about three superstitions in your country.
   There are a lot of / a few / not many superstitions in my country. Some people believe/think/say that … are lucky.

6 Work with partner. Talk about the superstitions. Do you believe that people can create their own luck?

Speaking Expressing surprise

Real talk: What are you afraid of?

1 **6.3** Watch the teenagers in the videos. How many teenagers …
   a) are afraid of animals?
   b) say they are not afraid of anything?
   c) are afraid of other things (not animals)?

2 What are *you* afraid of?

3 **2.22** Jack and Rosa are talking about a friend called Mike. What is he afraid of?

4 Complete the conversation with the useful language.

Useful language

What?
That can't be true!
You're joking!
That's impossible!
I don't believe you/it!
Are you serious?
No way!

Rosa:	Is Mike going to come sailing with us?
Jack:	No ¹ *way* ! He's terrified of deep water.
Rosa:	² …? That's ³ … ! He's a really good swimmer!
Jack:	No, it's true. He's got a phobia.
Rosa:	That ⁴ … true! He's competing in the 50 metre freestyle at the swimming club next week.
Jack:	I know, but he's scared of swimming in open water. I think it's because you can't see the bottom.
Rosa:	⁵ … serious? I didn't think Mike was scared of anything.
Jack:	Well, he's afraid of deep water. It's quite a common phobia, actually.
Rosa:	You're ⁶ … ! I've never heard of it.
Jack:	Mike told me himself.
Rosa:	I don't ⁷ … you! I'm going to call Mike and ask him.

5 **2.22** Listen again and check your answers.

6 Work with a partner. Practise the conversation in Exercise 4.

7 Work with a partner. Prepare a conversation like the one in Exercise 4. Use the photos below and the useful language. Practise the conversation with your partner.

Situation 1
You are going camping with some friends. Your friend Kevin has a phobia of spiders. He goes walking a lot, and loves sport.

Situation 2
You are going to go on a school trip to Rome. Your friend Donna is terrified of the dark. She is usually a confident person and speaks Italian!

Writing An email to a friend

1 Look at the photo and read Stefani's email. What is she worried about?

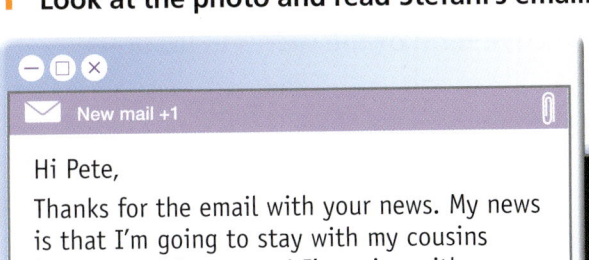

Hi Pete,

Thanks for the email with your news. My news is that I'm going to stay with my cousins in Norway this summer! I'm going with my parents and the idea is that we all go camping together. It's really exciting, but my problem is we're flying there! I've never been on a plane before and the truth is I'm really worried about flying. I don't know what to do! The fact is, when I think about flying over the sea, I feel tense and start sweating. It was embarrassing, but I had to tell my mum. She said it's just like going on a coach and told me not to worry. Not very helpful!

What do you think?

Regards,

Stefani

2 Read Stefani's email again. Put the information she writes about in order.
- explain the problem
- open email and say thanks for Pete's news *1*
- write about who she has spoken to about it
- describe how she feels and why
- ask for advice and close email
- give news and explain her plans

Useful language

Introducing news and explaining things
We can use different phrases to introduce what we want to say.
- *My news is (that) …*
- *… the idea is (that) …*

3 Look at the Useful language box. Find two other examples of introducing something in the email.

4 Complete the sentences using the words in brackets.
1 We're moving to Germany. (our news) *Our news is that we're moving to Germany.*
2 We stay there for two years. (the idea)
3 She doesn't want to go. (the truth)
4 A lot of people have this phobia. (the fact)
5 They visit me next year. (the idea)
6 I've got a dog. (my big news)

 Get writing

PLAN

5 Plan an email to a friend with your news and explaining a problem you have. Make notes on the things in Exercise 2.

WRITE

6 Write your email. Use your notes from Exercise 5 and the model text to help you.

CHECK

7 Can you say YES to these questions?
- Is the information from Exercise 2 in your email?
- Have you used expressions like *My news is that …* in your email?

5–6 Review

Vocabulary

1 Match the communication words with the comments.

> blog post   Tweet   forum   Skype™
> social media post   ~~text message~~

1 I can send short messages and it's cheaper than a phone call.   **text message**
2 I can chat with my friends and see them at the same time.
3 I can send really short messages to all my friends at the same time.
4 I can add photos and videos and my friends can visit my page.
5 I can ask questions and post messages and anyone on the list can reply.
6 I can write about my life and the things I'm interested in and anyone can read it.

2 Match the words with the definitions.

1 whisper   **c**   5 complain
2 boast   6 joke
3 criticise   7 shout
4 argue

a to say something is wrong
b to speak angrily with someone
c to talk very quietly
d to talk very loudly
e to say something funny
f to speak too proudly about something you have done
g to give a bad opinion about something

3 Match the sentences to the fears in the box.

> birds   clowns   lifts   ~~flying~~   the dark   snakes

1 I prefer taking the bus or train.   **flying**
2 I'll take the stairs.
3 I don't like them flying near me.
4 They can be poisonous and they move quickly.
5 They look frightening with their face and hair different colours.
6 Can you leave the light on?

4 Complete the sentences with the correct adjective form of the words in brackets.

1 Matthew feels really **tired** (tire).
2 Their new computer game is really .... (excite).
3 The TV programme was so .... (bore). I fell asleep.
4 Jason saw a spider and he was really .... (terrify).
5 Harry's book is really .... (interest).
6 Julie's test is tomorrow. She feels very .... (worry).

Explore vocabulary

5 Complete the text with the words in the box. Use the correct form of the phrasal verbs.

> virtual friends   come into use   get by
> ~~social network sites~~   turn into   face-to-face
> digital generation   personal information

The number of people using ¹ _social network sites_ is going up along with the number of ² .... that they have. In the past, we ³ .... with telephones and letters but the current ⁴ .... have access to different ways of communicating. Since computers, tablets and mobile phones have ⁵ ...., we have less ⁶ .... contact with friends and family and instead we prefer to give ⁷ .... for everyone to read. Are we ⁸ .... a generation of people who can't communicate with each other without a gadget?

6 Complete the sentences with *of*, *about* or *with*. Then write the opposite adjective of the underlined words.

1 Is that lift <u>safe</u>? I'm terrified **of** small spaces.   **dangerous**
2 What do you think .... this <u>old</u> mobile phone? It's enormous!
3 A: Ana won't share her <u>lucky</u> objects .... me.
   B: Well, you should find your own lucky things!
4 I'm really worried .... the exam. I saw a black cat too and that's <u>bad</u> luck!
5 A: Are you dressing up for the party?
   B: No, I'm embarrassed .... looking <u>silly</u>.

Language focus

1 Complete the sentences about life in the year 2050. Use *will*, *won't* or *might/may not*.
1. Everyone ..will.. use the Internet for shopping, I'm sure.
2. I think some schools .... offer classes on Skype™.
3. Cars .... use petrol, I'm sure. They'll be electric.
4. Lots of people .... probably work from home.
5. Robots .... definitely do all the housework – at least I hope so!
6. It's possible we .... read books anymore.

2 Complete the first conditional sentences. Use the verbs in brackets.
1. The librarian ..will be.. (be) upset if we ..talk.. (talk) too loudly in the library.
2. If you .... (not answer) my email, I .... (not write) to you ever again!
3. If we .... (get) Skype™, we .... (not pay) so much for our phone calls.
4. You .... (might win) the lottery if you .... (buy) a ticket.
5. You .... (not find out) what's happening in the world if you .... (not use) the Internet.
6. If she .... (have) her mobile with her, her mum .... (not worry) about her.
7. He .... (send) you a text message if he .... (hear) any news.
8. If he .... (work) hard enough, he .... (might win) a prize.

3 Complete the sentences with *be going to*, *will* or present continuous.
1. He ..is flying.. (fly) to Japan tomorrow.
2. Don't worry. He .... probably .... (call) you later.
3. My parents .... (take) me out for dinner on Saturday for my birthday.
4. What .... (you/do) when you leave school?
5. Sorry, but we .... (not see) you later – we have got a party to go to.
6. Susan .... (start) a new job on Monday.

4 Choose the correct words.

I had a terrible time at the concert last weekend. There were ¹ **too much / (too many)** people and there was ² **too much / too many** noise. There wasn't ³ **enough / a few** space in the hall and I felt quite scared. There were only ⁴ **a few / a little** windows and they were closed. I felt sick and I needed ⁵ **a few / a little** time to sit down and recover. There weren't ⁶ **too many / enough** chairs to sit on so luckily ⁷ **a few / too many** friends helped me. One friend asked me, '⁸ **How many / How much** concerts have you been to?' 'Lots!' I told her.

Language builder

5 Choose the correct words to complete the text.

Lisa:	Hi, Mike! I haven't seen you ¹ _a_ ages!
Mike:	I know! I ² .... on a trip to New York City and I ³ .... back. ⁴ .... been there?
Lisa:	No, I don't like big cities. There are usually ⁵ .... people and there's ⁶ .... noise.
Mike:	I love New York! If you ⁷ .... around the city you ⁸ .... some great places to eat and things to see. And I went to ⁹ .... jazz concerts, too.
Lisa:	Where ¹⁰ .... next?
Mike:	I'm not sure, I ¹¹ .... to Beijing and Shanghai.
Lisa:	That sounds great. If you go ¹² .... let me know?
Mike:	Sure!

	a	b	c
1	for	since	some
2	was going	have gone	went
3	was just coming	have just come	came just
4	Have you ever	Did you ever	Were you ever
5	too much	too many	a few
6	too much	too many	a little
7	walked	walk	have walked
8	find	are finding	will find
9	a little	a few	enough
10	you will visit	are you visiting	are you going to visit
11	might go	will go	'm going
12	I will	you will	will you

Speaking

6 Match the sentences.
1. You don't need to worry. _d_
2. That can't be true!
3. Listen, I think I can help you.
4. Are you serious?
5. Of course you can do it.
6. I don't believe you!

a. Well, why don't you ask him.
b. Thanks, but I'm really worried.
c. Yes, she's afraid of spiders.
d. I know, you're right.
e. Thanks, I feel more confident now.
f. I know, but it is.

7 School life

In this unit ...

The women of Ayoquesco **p77**

Playing with Maths **p80**

Asking for advice **p82**

CLIL Social media **p121**

Vocabulary
- Behaviour and discipline at school
- Words from the text
- *make* and *do*
- Phrasal verbs

Language focus
- Second conditional: affirmative and negative statements, *yes/no* questions
- Second conditional: *Wh-* questions

Unit aims
I can ...
- talk about behaviour and discipline at school.
- talk about imaginary situations.
- ask questions about imaginary situations.
- understand an article about teaching in Singapore.
- ask for and give advice.
- write a problem page.

BE CURIOUS

What can you see in the photo?

Start thinking
- What are the children doing?
- How important is your working environment at school?
- What are the best and worst parts of going to school?

Vocabulary Life at school

1 🔊 2.23 Match the words and phrases in the box with the photos (a–i). Then listen, check and repeat.

> bullying   hand in homework   get detention   ~~cheat in a test~~   be on time
> wear a uniform   write lines   scream or shout   get good marks

a *cheat in a test*

2 Look again at the phrases in Exercise 1. Which are bad or good behaviours and which are rules or punishments?

3 🔊 2.24 Listen to the conversation between David from the UK and Anita from Brazil about schools. Which things from Exercise 1 do they talk about?

Your turn

4 Work with a partner. Answer the questions.
1 Do you wear a uniform in your school? Why/Why not?
2 What do you think of cheating in tests?
3 Do you think your school is strict? Why/Why not?

We don't have to wear a uniform because …

I think cheating is bad because …

Our school is very strict because we always have to …

➡ **Vocabulary Bank** • page 113

Reading A student blog

1 Work with a partner. Look at the photo and answer the questions.
1. Where are the children?
2. Who are they?
3. What do you think they're discussing?

2 🔊 2.25 Read the article about a school in New York. In what ways is it different from other schools?

3 Read the article again. Are the sentences true or false? Correct the false ones.
1. The school has meetings every month. *F*
2. The students make suggestions and the teachers vote on their suggestions.
3. There are no rules.
4. The students can't choose their own subjects.
5. The teachers don't tell the students what to do.
6. Working in a team is very important at the Free School.

> 👁 **Get it right!**
>
> We use the infinitive after *want*.
> *If you want **to talk**, you have to put up your hand.*
> *I don't want **to do** the exam tomorrow!*

🔍 Explore words in context

4 Match the words and phrases from the article with the definitions (1–5) below.

> propose   vote   walk out   on our own   together

1. decide
2. alone – without other people
3. the opposite of alone
4. make a suggestion
5. leave a room without asking for permission

💬 Your turn

5 Answer the questions. Make notes.
1. Would you like to go to a school like the Brooklyn Free School? Why/Why not?
2. What rules would you change in your school? Why?
3. What subjects would you like to study that you don't already study? Why?

6 Discuss your answers in groups.

I'd really like/love/hate to go to a school like this.
I'd like to change the rule about … because it's …
I'd really like to study … . I think it's important/ interesting because …

BROWN'S FREE SCHOOL

This week's student blogger is a new student, Jacklyn Whyte.

A lot of people are asking me about my new school. It's really hard to explain, so I give them an example of one day.

It's Wednesday morning and it's time for the weekly school meeting. This week, one of the topics is 'wheels'. Kyle, one of the kids in my class, proposes a new rule that students can bring skateboards, skates and bicycles to school. Our teacher, Mr Jackson, suggests that we do this one day a week and the whole school votes on a 'wheels' day for next Friday.

If I wanted to change the rules at my old school, it wouldn't be that easy! But here at the Brown's Free School, things are different. Here, *we* make the decisions! We can decide to go to class, watch TV or play a computer game, but most students choose to go to class – it's more interesting! When we don't like a class, we just walk out! In my old school, if I didn't stay until the end of a class, I'd be in detention!

At the Free School, the teachers don't give detention, and no one writes lines. There's no uniform and there are no exams. We choose what we want to study and how. We can work in groups, or study on our own. If you were at the school and you wanted to study car mechanics, our teachers would help you find a way to study it. If you wanted to start a new school magazine, you would suggest it to the teachers. Then, they would find a way to help you do it.

That's how the Free School works. The ideas come from the students and everyone works together to make them happen. It's a great experience and I love going to the Free School!

add a comment | send a message

> **FACT!** *Although the USA has the most free schools in the world, many other countries have free schools too, including Brazil, India, Japan, the UK and Germany.*

Language focus 1 Second conditional

1 Complete the examples from the text on page 76. Then complete the rules.

imaginary situation	possible consequence
If I .... until the end of a class,	I .... in detention!
If you .... to start a new school magazine,	you .... it to the teachers.

1 We use .... + past simple and .... + infinitive to form the second conditional.
2 We use the second conditional to talk about unreal situations in the present or **future / past**.

→ Grammar reference • page 105

2 Look at the chart. Choose the correct form of the verbs in the sentences below.
1 If I **was** / 'd be rude to a teacher, I **got** / **'d get** detention.
2 If I **didn't / wouldn't** pass my exams, my parents **didn't / wouldn't** be very happy!
3 If a teacher **gave / would give** me lines, I **wrote / 'd write** them during the break.
4 My teacher **called / would call** my parents if I **didn't / wouldn't** go to school.
5 My friends **did / would** like to go to the Free School if they **opened / would open** one in our town.
6 I **didn't / wouldn't** study Maths if I **went / would go** to the Free School.

3 Write complete sentences.
1 If I / go / to the Free School / not study Maths
   If I went to the Free School, I wouldn't study Maths.
2 If I / not do homework / my teacher / give / detention
3 If I / not study English / not know / how to do this exercise
4 I / tell / my parents / if / there / be / bullying in my school
5 I / do / art in class / if / have the choice
6 I / not get / good marks / if / not study every day

→ Say it right! • page 97

Your turn

4 Read the quiz and choose answers for you.

1	**If I came home late one night, …**
a	my parents would be very angry.
b	my parents wouldn't say anything.
c	I'd get some kind of punishment.

2	**If I was rude to one of my parents, …**
a	I'd feel bad and I'd say sorry immediately.
b	they'd be very shocked because I'm never rude.
c	they'd punish me with no TV or computer for a week.

3	**If I borrowed something from my brother/sister/friend without asking, …**
a	it wouldn't be a problem. They do it to me all the time!
b	they'd tell my parents and I'd get into a lot of trouble!
c	I'd put it back before they noticed.

5 Compare your quiz answers with your partner.

If I came home late, I'd get some kind of punishment. I wouldn't go out for two or three weeks.

Learn about a successful business.
• What happened in Ayoquezco in 1979?
• What do people use prickly pear for?
• What did the women decide to do?

7.1 The women of Ayoquezco

Listening A discussion

1 🔊 **2.28** Listen to the quiz. Put the pictures in the correct order.

2 🔊 **2.28** Listen again and choose the correct answers.

1 If Mick saw a classmate cheating in an exam, he would …
  a say nothing and just continue with his work.
  b tell a teacher.
  c try to cheat as well.
2 If Suzy found a wallet full of money on the street near her school, she would …
  a take it to the nearest police station.
  b give it to a teacher at the school.
  c keep it.
3 What is Mick more careful about now?
  a Not losing his mobile phone.
  b What he tells his dad.
  c Who he gives his phone number to.
4 If someone sent Suzy some horrible messages on her phone she would …
  a show them to her parents.
  b do nothing.
  c tell the police.

3 Work with a partner. Discuss what you would do in the situations in Exercise 3.

Vocabulary make and do

4 🔊 **2.29** Match the words in the box to the verbs, *make* or *do*. Then listen, check and repeat.

> ~~your homework~~   ~~a mistake~~   friends   a noise
> an exercise   a phone call   something interesting
> a mess   the right thing   decision

do your homework ….
make a mistake ….

➡ **Vocabulary Bank** • page 113

Your turn

5 Complete the questions with the correct verb *make* or *do* then answer the questions. Make notes.
  1 Do you find it easy to …. friends?
  2 How many hours of homework do you …. every week?
  3 How do you feel when you …. a mistake in class?
  4 Does your mum get angry with you when you …. a mess in your room?

6 Ask and answer with your partner.

I find it easy to make friends because I'm not very shy.

Language focus 2 Second conditional questions

1 Complete the examples from the listening on page 78.

Wh- questions	
What **would** you do **if** you saw someone cheating? **If** you found a wallet, what .... you do?	
Yes/No questions	**Short answers**
.... someone **sent** you horrible messages on your phone would you tell a teacher? **Would** you tell your parents **if** you **failed** an exam?	Yes, I/you/he/she/it/we/they would. No, I/you/he/she/it/we/they wouldn't.

➡ Grammar reference • page 105

2 Look at the chart. Choose the correct words to complete the sentences.
1 What did / (would) you do if you (were) / would be the head teacher of your school?
2 If your best friend didn't / wouldn't invite you to his/her birthday, what did / would you say?
3 If your family lived / would live in an English-speaking country, did / would your lives be very different?
4 What job did / would your teacher do if he/she wasn't / wouldn't be a teacher?
5 If your grandparents lived / would live in the USA, did / would you go to visit them?

3 🔊 2.30 Complete the conversation with the correct form of the verbs in brackets. Then listen and check.

A: Can I ask you a few questions?
B: Yes, sure.
A: OK, first question: what ¹ _would_ you .... (do) if you ² .... (win) a TV talent show?
B: Wow! I think I'd have a huge party with all my friends and family!
A: And if you ³ .... (have) a party, where ⁴ .... you .... (have) it?
B: I'd definitely have it on a beach, if I could!
A: OK, second question. If you ⁵ .... (can) be famous, what ⁶ .... you .... (be)?
B: I don't know. I'd like to be a singer maybe.
A: OK. Last question. If you ⁷ .... (not have to) go to school, what ⁸ .... you .... (do) all day?
B: That's easy! I'd play my guitar, listen to music and spend time with my friends!
A: Thank you!

Your turn

4 Answer the questions. Make notes.

1 If you had a million pounds, what would you buy?
2 If you ruled the world, what would you change?
3 If you didn't have to go to school, what would you do all day?
4 If you could learn a musical instrument, which instrument would you learn?
5 If you weren't a teenager, what age would you like to be?
6 If you were 18, what would you do that you can't do now?

5 Ask and answer the questions in Exercise 4 with your partner.

Let me think. OK, if I had a million pounds, I'd buy a really big house by the sea!

Discover Culture

1 **Work with a partner. Look at the photos and answer the questions.**
   1 Which class looks more fun? Why?
   2 Do you like Maths? Why/Why not? What kinds of things do you do in your Maths class?

Find out about learning Maths.

7.2 Playing with Maths

2 ▶ 7.2 **Watch the video without sound. Try to answer the questions.**
   1 How do we use Maths in everyday life?
   2 What is the first group of pupils learning about? (0.27–1.09)
   3 What is the second group of pupils learning about? (1.10–2.30)

3 ▶ 7.2 **Watch the video with sound and check your answers.**

4 ▶ 7.2 **Watch the video with sound and complete the sentences.**
   1 Students either love or …. Maths.
   2 We use Maths to measure distance, design art work, go shopping and ….
   3 Students get into groups to learn about ….
   4 Students do …. to learn about shapes in Maths.
   5 The students find geometric shapes in different ….
   6 Learning Maths this way is interesting and ….

5 **Test your visual memory about what the students do. Are these statements true or false? If false, correct them.**
   1 There is a student running in a race at the start.
   2 The first groups of students do the fractions game in pairs.
   3 The students in the Art/Maths class sit on chairs in front of the teacher.
   4 The students have to discover geometry in art.
   5 They write down a list of the different shapes on the board.

6 **What objects do you see in the video? How is each one used in the Maths class?**

> marbles   a mouse (computer)   smartphone
> a quilt   a clock   small stones   a football

a mouse – we use Maths when we use a computer

Your turn

7 **Ask and answer with your partner.**
   1 Which of the two Maths lessons in the video do you like the most? Why?
   2 When do you use Maths outside class? Do your classes help with these things? Why/Why not?
   I use Maths when I …
   We don't need maths class for everyday life, we have calculators.

Reading An article

1 Work with a partner. Look at the photo of Singapore and make a list of at least three adjectives to describe the city.

2 🔊 2.31 Read the article about Singapore. What's the main focus of the article?
   a The location and geography of the country
   b Learning languages in Singapore
   c A new way of teaching an old subject

3 Read the article again and answer the questions.
   1 Where is Singapore?
   2 What is special about the country?
   3 Is the Singapore approach to teaching Maths a traditional Asian approach?
   4 At what age do children start school in Singapore?
   5 How do children learn basic ideas in Maths in Singapore?
   6 Which countries have adopted the Singapore approach?

Explore phrasal verbs

4 Look at the highlighted words in the text. Match the phrasal verbs in the box with the definitions (1–5).

> pick up   find out   write out   work out   try out

   1 write something again more completely
   2 do the calculation to find an answer to Maths problem
   3 learn something new
   4 test something to see if it works
   5 get information about something or learn about it

➡ Vocabulary Bank • page 113

Your turn

5 Compare the primary school with yours. Write sentences. Compare your sentences with your partner.

	classroom atmosphere	learning things
Singapore		
My school		

Singapore
A SUCCESS STORY

Singapore is a fascinating place. It's a giant floating city 130 kilometres north of the Equator. The city has four official languages – Chinese, Malay, Tamil and English. English is the language everyone uses for official business and all the schools teach English.

Singapore is one of the smallest countries in the world, but it is also one of the richest. For years, it has been famous for its high level of education – and it's the number one country in the world for teaching Maths. Most people think that Asian schools in general are very strict. Is this the secret of Singapore's great success too? Not at all! If you walked into a Maths class in a primary school in Singapore, you'd be surprised by how active and noisy it was. You wouldn't see children sitting quietly in their chairs watching their teacher at the board and **writing out** sums in their notebooks. You would see a lot of activity and hear a lot of noise.

School starts at the age of seven in Singapore. The Maths programme starts very slowly and the younger children spend a lot of time on the first steps. They use everyday objects, like beans and fruit, to feel and see the basic ideas. They don't copy from the board or do exercises in their books – they **pick** Maths **up** through playing. By sharing objects with friends, they **find out** about division. By building towers with blocks, they learn addition. It looks like the children are simply playing, but they're not – they're **working out** the answers to complex problems in a fun and interesting way.

Would this system work if it was taught in your country? A lot of schools around the world have **tried** it **out** – the UK for example, and the USA. And it's been a great success.

FACT! The largest Maths class was given in Nigeria in July 2013 with 2,381 people in the class.

Speaking Asking for and giving advice

Real talk: Who would you talk to if you needed advice?

1 **7.3** Watch the teenagers in the video. How many teenagers …
   a) would talk to a member of their family?
   b) would talk to a friend?
   c) say they would get good advice?

2 Who would *you* talk to if you needed advice?

3 **2.32** Hayley is talking to her friend James. What does Hayley want advice about?

4 Complete the conversation with the useful language.

Useful language

What's the problem?
I need your advice.
It's a good idea to …
What do you think I should do?
If I were you I wouldn't …
Maybe we could …
Have you tried …?
They say I shouldn't worry.

Hayley:	James, can I talk to you? I ¹ *need your* advice.
James:	Yes, of course. What's ² … ?
Hayley:	Well, there's a girl in my class who is saying nasty things about me.
James:	Really? What sort of things?
Hayley:	Oh, that I copy her homework and cheat in exams. It's awful! What do you think ³ … do?
James:	Look, if I were you, I ⁴ … listen to her. What do your other friends say?
Hayley:	They say I ⁵ … worry. But I can't help it.
James:	Yeah. Perhaps it's ⁶ … idea to do something.
Hayley:	Yes, but what?
James:	Well, have you ⁷ … talking to her? Maybe we ⁸ … do it together.
Hayley:	Yes, that's a good idea. Thanks, James!

5 **2.32** Listen again and check your answers.

6 Work with a partner. Practise the conversation in Exercise 4.

7 Work with a partner. Prepare a conversation like the one in Exercise 4. Use the photos below and the useful language. Practise the conversation with your partner.

Problem 1
Someone in your class has taken your mobile phone. (nobody knows who)

Problem 2
You have lost two text books you left in the classroom yesterday.

Writing A problem page

1 Read Paula's letter. What is the problem?

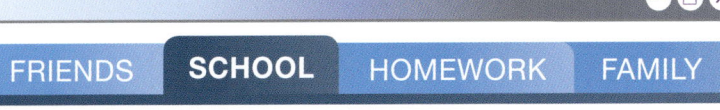

FRIENDS | SCHOOL | HOMEWORK | FAMILY

My English teacher hates me!
Paula asked 4 days ago

Hi everyone

I need some advice. I think my teacher hates me. I've had detention every week for the last four weeks from Mr Harris, my English teacher. English was always my best subject and Mr Harris was my favourite teacher, but now I'm not getting good marks. He's always giving me detention. What should I do?

best answer
LiverpoolLad answered 2 days ago

I think maybe the problem is not only your teacher but also your marks. You say that English was your best subject and that your marks haven't been very good recently. Perhaps your English teacher is strict because he wants to show you that he's not happy with your marks. It's possible that he's trying to make you work harder by giving you detention.

I think you should try talking to him because communication is always the best way to work out a solution to a problem. You should ask him what the problem is and why you are getting detention. You could also work harder to improve your marks.

I really hope this helps.

2 Read the answer from LiverpoolLad again. What things does he do in his answer?
- Give a title
- Say what he thinks the real problem might be
- Give reasons for his opinions
- Offer different ways of looking at the problem
- Give direct orders
- Offer several solutions
- Give reasons for his advice
- Write a final sentence to make the person feel better

Useful language

Summarising a problem and giving advice
Use different phrases to summarise what you want to say and to give advice.
- I think maybe the problem is not only … but also …
- You say that …
- I think you should try … because …

3 Look at the Useful language box. Find two other phrases to give advice in Exercise 1.

4 Complete the sentences with the words in the box.

> should   try   problem   possible
> Perhaps   also

1. I think maybe the …. is your marks. …. your teacher is angry with you. It's …. that he wants to encourage you.
2. You …. talk to him. I think you should …. asking him for advice. You could …. study harder.

PLAN

5 Read the problem below. Plan your answer. Make notes on the things in Exercise 2.

> Isabel cheated in a Maths test. It was the first time and she feels bad. She didn't study and she wrote the answers on her arm. She got a good mark and her parents are going to buy her a new mobile.

WRITE

6 Write your answer. Use your notes from Exercise 5 and the model text to help you.

CHECK

7 Can you say YES to these questions?
- Is the information from the plan in your answer?
- Have you used different expressions to restate the problem and to give your advice?

8 Green planet

Discovery EDUCATION

In this unit ...

Where does it all go? **p87**

Build it better **p90**

Doing voluntary work **p92**

CLIL Driving into the future **p122**

Vocabulary
- Materials
- Words from the text
- Energy issues
- Phrasal verbs

Language focus
- Present simple passive
- Past simple passive

Unit aims
I can ...
- talk about types of materials.
- describe how materials are recycled.
- talk about the energy I use at home.
- understand a text about renewable energy.
- apologise and explain to a friend.
- write a newspaper article.

BE CURIOUS
What can you see in the photo?
Start thinking
- What is a wind farm?
- What do wind turbines produce?
- Why are they good for the environment?

Vocabulary Materials

1 🔊 2.33 Match a material (or materials) in the box with objects in the photos. Then listen, check and repeat. What's the function of each of the objects?

> bricks   cement   cotton   glass   leather   metal   paper   plastic   rubber   ~~wood~~

a *wood*

2 Match the materials from Exercise 1 with the sentences.
1. We often use this material to make furniture like chairs and tables. *wood*
2. We often use this material to make shoes, bags, and belts.
3. If you drop a bottle made of this material, it will probably break.
4. This material is very common for making T-shirts.
5. We make tyres for cars with this material.
6. This is the most common material used to make books.
7. These two materials are very common for building houses.

👁 Get it right!
We don't use *the* before plural nouns to talk about things in a general way. ✓
We often use this material to make *the* shoes. ✗

3 🔊 2.34 Listen to the conversation. Complete the chart with the things they talk about.

leather	shoes
cotton	
glass	
wood	
paper	
rubber	
plastic	
metal	

Your turn

4 Think of two objects you've got at home for each of the materials in Exercise 1. Make notes. Work with a partner. Tell him/her about the objects.

I've got a lot of leather shoes.

➡ **Vocabulary Bank** • page 114

➡ **Say it right!** • page 97

Reading An article

1 Work with a partner. Look at the pictures and answer the questions.
1. What are the people building?
2. What materials are they using?
3. Why are they using them?

2 🔊 2.37 Read an article about Mike Reynolds. What kind of houses does he build?

3 Read the article again and answer the questions.
1. How does Mike protect his Earthships from the cold?
2. How does he provide light during the day?
3. Why does he grow his plants in the front of the house?
4. How does he get energy and water?
5. How did he and his organisation help other people?
6. What is Mike's main message to the world?

Explore words in context

4 Match the verbs in the box with the definitions (1–7).

> warrior   throw away   shaped   match
> decoration   northern   reuse

1. made into a particular form or shape
2. use again
3. someone who fights for something
4. be similar to or look the same
5. put something in the rubbish
6. things used to make something look beautiful
7. from the north

Your turn

5 Which materials do you recycle or reuse at school or at home? What do you do with them? Makes notes.

6 Talk about your notes from Exercise 5. Is it easy to recycle materials in your area? Why/Why not?

At school, we recycle some of our rubbish.
My mum takes plastic stuff to a special container.
It's very easy to recycle materials where I live. There's a container for every type of rubbish.

GARBAGE WARRIOR

Mike Reynolds builds houses from recycled materials to show us what we waste. Mike's houses are built using the things that other people throw away. His Earthships (as his houses are called) are beautiful buildings. They are shaped and coloured to match the landscape around them. He uses bottles to create beautiful walls full of light. There are plants everywhere, inside and out. But the plants and the bottles, like everything else in the Earthships, are not only there for decoration. Every single material in an Earthship is carefully chosen. Old car tyres are used to build strong walls. The rubber protects the houses from the cold northern winds in winter. These walls are built at the back of the house. The walls at the front of the house are built from metal cans or glass bottles. They're held together with the earth from around them and cement is not used at all. The beautiful bottle walls are built to the south to give light during the day. The house is heated by the larger front windows. They also create the perfect temperature for growing all kinds of fruit and vegetables, and the plants are protected against the bad weather. When you live in an Earthship, you grow your own food, get electricity from the sun and wind and you get water from the rain and snow.

Mike and the Earthship organisation use their ability and experience to help people all over the world. In 2010, they visited victims of the earthquake in Haiti. They taught them how to build safe, new homes quickly and cheaply from materials that they could find around them. Mike points out that rubbish only exists because we humans create it. That is exactly what Mike, the Garbage Warrior, wants us to see – that we have to stop waste and reuse our rubbish.

Mike Reynolds builds houses from recycled materials.

An Earthship home. These houses are a symbol of his fight against waste.

FACT! Recycled tyres are used to build roads and pavements.

Language focus 1 Present simple passive

1 Complete the examples from the text on page 86. Then complete the rules.

+	Old car tyres …. …. to build walls. The house …. …. by the larger front windows.
–	Cement …. …. . Mike's houses **are not built** with traditional materials.

1 To form the passive, use …. + past participle.
2 Active: They make the houses from rubbish.
3 Passive: The houses …. from rubbish.

➡ Grammar reference • page 106

2 Look at the chart. Complete the sentences. Use the passive form of the verbs in brackets.
1 The house (make) of bottles and cans.
   The house is made of bottles and cans.
2 The cans (recycle) to build walls.
3 The walls (design) to protect the house from extreme temperatures.
4 The heat from the sun (use) to give power to the house.
5 The water from the kitchen (reuse) in the garden.
6 The houses (build) into the side of a hill.

👁 Get it right!
Passive not active
The houses **are called** Earthships.
The town **is located** in the south.
Active not passive
The Art lesson **starts** at 10 o'clock. (not ~~is started~~)
The exhibition **closes** today. (not ~~is closed~~)

3 🔊 2.38 Choose the correct words to complete the text. Then listen and check.

Rows and rows of human statues are standing in the main square. As you ¹ **move / are moved** closer, you ² **see / are seen** that they ³ **make / are made** of all kinds of everyday objects. Some ⁴ **build / are built** from plastic bags, bottles and cans. Others ⁵ **decorate / are decorated** with computer keyboards or TV screens. The Trash Army, as it ⁶ **call / is called**, is a travelling exhibition. It has travelled all over the world and it ⁷ **shows / is shown** people how much rubbish we ⁸ **produce / is produced** through our modern lifestyles.

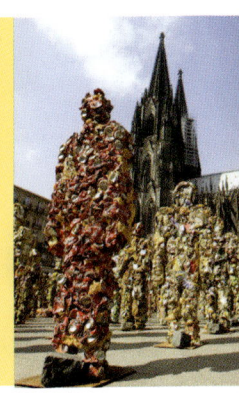

Present simple passive questions

4 Look at the questions about the text on page 86 and complete the rule.
• **Are** the walls in Mike's house **made** of bricks?
• Why **are** rubber tyres **used**?
• What **are** the walls at the front of the house **made** from?
• **Is** the house **heated** by electricity?

To form questions we use …. + subject + …. .

5 Answer the questions in Exercise 4 about the text.

6 Order the questions.
1 your / wood / house / is / made of?
2 recycled / the plastic bottles / your / are / in / house?
3 for / later / newspapers and magazines / old / are / saved?
4 reused / plastic bags / are?
5 your / vegetables / are / grown / garden / in?

🔴 Your turn

7 Ask and answer the questions in Exercise 6.
A: *Is your house made of wood?*
B: *No, it isn't. It's made of bricks.*

A bathroom

Learn about rubbish in the sea.
• What sort of rubbish do you think is found in the sea?
• Why is the sea so important for the planet?
• What happens to rubbish in the sea?

Discovery EDUCATION
8.1 Where does it all go?

Listening A class presentation

1 Work with a partner. Look at the picture of a living room and say how the room is similar to and different from the living room in your home.

2 🔊 2.39 The living room is an exhibit in a museum. Listen to three students talking about the house. What do they talk about?
a Heating homes in the past
b Changing technology at home
c Energy at home

3 🔊 2.39 Listen again and answer the questions.
1 How long has the Eco House been open?
2 What does the museum use the Eco House for?
3 What does Rebecca say about computers?
4 What uses the most energy?
5 What did the experiment show?
6 What does the last student want to discuss about the house?

Vocabulary Energy issues

4 Match the verbs from the class presentation with the definitions (1–7).

> consume   leave on standby   switch off   waste
> save energy   turn down   reduce

1 to use energy
2 to stop energy being wasted
3 to use more energy than you need
4 to make something smaller
5 to leave an appliance connected to the electricity
6 to disconnect an appliance from the electricity
7 you use less energy by doing this with an appliance

5 🔊 2.40 Complete the sentences with the correct form of the verbs in Exercise 4. Then listen and check.
1 Don't forget to ..*switch off*.. the lights before you go to bed.
2 Can you .... the heating? It's really warm.
3 You shouldn't .... the TV .... at night.
4 Did you know your computer .... a lot of electricity?
5 It's better to have a shower than a bath because you don't .... so much water.
6 You should try to .... the number of hours you use the air conditioning.
7 We're trying to .... so I always switch off my computer when I'm not using it.

Your turn

6 Ask and answer with your partner.
1 How do you save energy in your house?
2 How do you think you could save more energy at home?
3 Why is it important to save energy?

I always switch of my computer and the monitor before I go to bed.
I leave the TV on standby so I should switch it off.
Saving energy is important for the environment.

➤ Vocabulary Bank • page 114

Language focus 2

Past simple passive

1 Complete the examples from the listening on page 88.

+	The Eco house .... **built** in 1985. Several changes .... **made** to the house.
–	A lot of rubbish .... **recycled** in the 1980s. The lights **were not** switched off for a week.
with *by*	The Eco house **was designed by** the museum.

➔ Grammar reference • page 106

2 Complete the sentences. Use the past simple passive form of the verbs in brackets.
1. The Eco house ...*was completed*... (complete) in 1985.
2. It .... (build) on a large piece of land.
3. A lot of energy .... (save) by turning down the temperature.
4. The kitchen .... (redesign) two years ago.
5. A lot of changes .... (make) to the house.
6. The old fridge and washing machine .... (not throw) away.

3 Write the active sentences below using the past passive and *by*.
1. Companies first used plastic bottles in 1947.
   Plastic bottles were first used in 1947.
2. They finished the Burj Al Arab hotel in Dubai in 1999.
3. The Chinese invented paper almost 2,000 years ago.
4. Europeans threw out about 100 million mobile phones last year.
5. Swiss people recycled 96% of glass bottles in 2012.
6. John Dunlop made the first rubber tyre for his son's bicycle.

Past simple passive questions

4 Complete the examples from the listening on page 88.

Wh- questions
Why .... the Eco house ....? When **was** the house **completed**?
Yes/No questions and short answers
.... a lot of energy .... by reducing the temperature? Yes, it **was**./No, it **wasn't**. **Were** the lights **switched** off last night? Yes, they **were**./No, they **weren't**.

➔ Grammar reference • page 106

5 🔊 **2.41** Complete the conversation with the correct form of the past simple passive. Then listen and check.

A: Hey, shall we do this general knowledge quiz?
B: OK. But I'm not very good!
A: OK, first question. ¹.... *Don Quixote* ².... (write) by Shakespeare?
B: That's easy! No, it ³..... It ⁴.... by Cervantes.
A: Good! Question two – ⁵.... the first modern Olympic Games ⁶.... (hold) in Greece?
B: No, they ⁷..... They ⁸.... in London.
A: No, it was Athens! OK, the last question – again it's very easy! Who ⁹.... Harry Potter ¹⁰.... (play) by?
B: I know that one! He ¹¹.... by Daniel Radcliffe – easy!

Your turn

6 Write five general knowledge quiz questions using the past passive. Use the questions in Exercises 5 and 6 to help.

In the Spider Man films, who was Spider Man's girlfriend played by?

7 Ask and answer your questions with your partner. Give full sentences.

A: *In the Spider Man films, who was Spider Man's girlfriend played by?*
B: *She was played by Emma Stone.*

Discover Culture

1 Work with a partner. Look at the photos and describe them. What do you think the video will be about?

Find out about building sustainably.

8.2 Build it better

2 ▶ 8.2 Watch the video without sound and check your ideas.

3 Which of the words below do you think you will hear in the video?

> tornado   flood   sustainable   renewable
> sunlight   rain   mirror   solar panels   natural
> electricity   environment

4 ▶ 8.2 Watch the video with sound. Check your answers to Exercise 3.

5 ▶ 8.2 Watch the video again and match the information.

1	hail stones	a	of homes and businesses destroyed
2	95%	b	Greensburg was created
3	the wind speed was	c	create energy for the building
4	the solar panels	d	the size of tennis balls
5	a new and improved	e	320 km per hour

6 Complete the text about rebuilding Greensburg. Use the words in the box.

> mirror   holes   solar panels   tubes   sunlight
> building   sustainable   electricity   heat

Solar energy was used in the new building. ¹.... shines into these tubes. It's reflected through the tubes by a ².... and it lights up the room. A special cover on top of each tube keeps the ³.... outside. Then large ⁴.... were made and the ⁵.... were placed inside them. For even more ⁶.... energy ⁷.... were built. When the panels receive sunlight, they turn it into ⁸..... Solar panels can create enough energy to power the whole ⁹.....

7 ▶ 8.2 Watch the video again and check your answers to Exercises 5 and 6.

Your turn

8 Discuss the questions in groups.
1 What are the most common natural disasters in your country?
2 Are there any buildings in your town with solar panels?
3 Do many people have solar panels on their houses in your town?
4 Do you think solar panels are a good idea? Why/Why not?

In my country, we have terrible forest fires ...

Reading An article

1 Work with a partner. Look at the photos and answer the questions.
   1 What can you see in each photo?
   2 What connects the photos?

2 🔊 2.42 Read the article about renewable energy. Match the renewable energies in the photos with the countries in the text.

3 Read the article again and answer the questions.
   1 Where does Minnesota get its biomass from?
   2 What two benefits does using biomass have for the environment?
   3 Why is the sun so important in Australia?
   4 What two results has the use of solar power had in Australia?
   5 Why has Britain got lots of sea and wind?
   6 Which wind farm will produce more electricity?

Explore phrasal verbs

4 Look at the highlighted words in the text. Match the phrasal verbs (1–5) with the definitions (a–e).
   1 bring down   a build
   2 keep on   b cut so it falls to the ground
   3 put up   c reduce/make smaller
   4 knock down   d fall to the ground
   5 cut down   e continue

➡ Vocabulary Bank • page 114

Your turn

5 Make notes about the questions.
   1 Why is renewable energy important for our world?
   2 What renewable energy is used in your country?
   3 What do you do to save energy at home or at school?

6 Ask and answer the questions in Exercise 5 with your partner. Use your notes to help you.

THREE COUNTRIES, THREE RENEWABLES

Humans are capable of producing energy that – unlike oil, natural gas and coal – do not damage the environment. We look at three countries and three different renewable energy sources.

The USA
The USA has several renewable energy projects. A lot of power stations use biomass to produce energy. Biomass is anything natural – plants and trees mostly – and it can be used to produce electricity. In a recent storm in Minnesota, over 3,000 trees were **knocked down** by strong winds. The wood from the trees was burned to produce energy. The state also wants to **cut down** 40,000 more trees because they are diseased. Of course, new trees are planted in place of the old ones, which also helps the environment.

Australia
It's certainly sunny in Australia. The country gets more than 3,500 hours of sunlight a year – that's ten hours a day – and solar energy is big business. Australia has spent a lot of money on solar energy. Solar panels power houses, schools, businesses and factories all over the country. About a quarter of all homes in South Australia use solar power. Australian solar power has **brought down** the country's energy bills and has had a very positive environmental effect. If Australia **keeps on** spending money on energy, it is thought that by 2030, 100% of Australia's energy could come from renewable sources.

The UK
Everyone knows that in the UK it's not sunny very often! Britain only gets between 1,200 and 1,600 hours of sunlight a year. So it's clear that solar power isn't big in Britain. But Britain has other renewable sources that can produce energy. It's an island so the British government is taking advantage of the often windy conditions and is **putting up** wind farms off its coasts. In Cumbria, in the north-west of England, enough energy is produced by more than 100 turbines to power over 320,000 homes. On the other side of the country, there is a wind farm with 88 wind turbines off the coast of Norfolk.

FACT! The Earth gets enough sunlight in one hour to give energy to the whole world for one year.

Speaking Apologising and explaining

Real talk: Do you do any volunteer work?

1 ▶ 8.3 Watch the teenagers in the video. Which volunteer work do they do?
- babysitting
- help in after-school clubs
- cleaning the school
- read to older people
- pick up litter
- teach children English
- help in school garden
- help older people with their animals

2 💬 Do *you* do any volunteer work?

3 🔊 2.43 Jessica meets her friend Oliver. How many excuses does Jessica give?

4 Complete the conversation with the useful language.

Useful language

I'm really sorry.
I'm sorry.
I really meant to come, honest!
I completely forgot.

Oh well, never mind.
The thing is, …
I'll (come next week), I promise.
The problem was, …

5 🔊 2.43 Listen again and check your answers.

6 💬 Work with a partner. Practise the conversation in Exercise 4.

7 💬 Change the words in bold in the conversation. Use the information below. Take turns to apologise to a friend and explain what the problem was.

Oliver: Hello Jessica. What happened to you **yesterday**?
Jessica: **Yesterday**? What do you mean?
Oliver: We were **planting vegetables in the school garden**.
Jessica: Oh, yes! I'm ¹…… *sorry* …… I completely ²…… .
Oliver: Jessica, I **sent you a text** to remind you!
Jessica: Yes, I know, I really ³…… to come, honest! The problem ⁴…… **my alarm clock was broken**.
Oliver: Well it was only **a couple of hours, not all day**.
Jessica: Yes, I know. I ⁵…… sorry, Oliver. ⁶…… is, I had a lot of chores to do too and because I slept late, I didn't have time.
Oliver: Oh well, ⁷…… mind. How about **next week**? We're planning to **plant some fruit trees**.
Jessica: Great! I'll come **next week**, ⁸…… !

Situation 1
You forgot to go with your friend to see an exhibition about Earthships. Now your friend is angry.

Situation 2
You didn't help your friend write an article about recycling. Now your friend is angry.

✏️ Writing A newspaper article

1 Look at the photos and read the article from a school newspaper. What did the volunteers do?

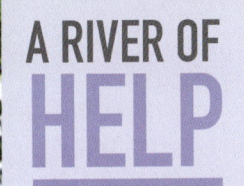

A RIVER OF HELP

LAST SUNDAY ABOUT 100 PEOPLE WENT TO LONGLEY NATURE RESERVE TO CLEAN UP THE RIVER. *THE EVENT* WAS ORGANISED BY THE CLEANUPRIVERS PROJECT, WHICH HELPS TO PROTECT THE ENVIRONMENT.

'Every summer local volunteers collect rubbish which is thrown in the river,' John Sanders, from Cleanuprivers told me. This time I was one of them. We picked up hundreds of plastic bottles, food packets and drinks cans. But that's not all that's in the river. 'We also found car tyres, a fridge and an old bed!' one volunteer said.

The clean-up also removes non-native plants from the river. These plants kill off native species and affect biodiversity. At Longley we cut down Himalayan Balsam. 'It's a beautiful plant, but dangerous because it covers everything,' said the local plant expert, Lynn Douglas. The clean-up was hard work but fun, and the river looked great! So when is the next event? Check the Cleanuprivers.org web page.

Report by Chris Davies

2 Read the newspaper article again. Put the information in the correct order.
- What is happening next?
- When did they do it? *1*
- What did they do?
- What was the opinion of the event?
- Who was involved?

Useful language

Using direct speech
When writing newspaper articles, use direct quotes.
'Every summer, ... in the river,' John Sanders ... told me.

3 Look at the Useful language box. Find more examples of direct speech in the text. What is the punctuation for exclamations?

4 Write these direct speech sentences with the correct punctuation.
1 What happened to the river she asked
   'What happened to the river?' she asked.
2 It's amazing said Abby
3 Meet me at the river she told me
4 We have to clear out all this rubbish she said
5 Are you coming to the next event I asked Tom

✏️ Get writing

PLAN

5 Plan your newspaper article about an event (sport, cultural) in your area. Make notes on the things in Exercise 2 and use the same structure.

WRITE

6 Write your essay. Use your notes from Exercise 5 and the model text to help you.

CHECK

7 Can you say YES to these questions?
- Is the information from the plan in your article?
- Have you used some direct speech in your article?

7–8 Review

Vocabulary

1 Complete the text with the correct form of the words in the box.

> bullying   hand in homework   get detention
> cheat in a test   on time   ~~wear a uniform~~
> get good marks   write lines

I like my school but there are a few rules that we have to follow. We have to ¹ _wear a uniform_ – it's a white shirt and a black skirt or trousers. In the morning, if you aren't ² …. , you have to write your name in the late book. We have to ³ …. on Friday morning – we get it twice a week. If we forget we ⁴ …. – this means we have to stay after school and ⁵ …. . I study hard and I usually ⁶ …. . I've never ⁷ …. and anyone who tries to cheat gets into trouble. All the students in my school are kind and friendly – there's no ⁸ …. – it's a great school.

2 Complete the phrases with *make* or *do*.
1 _make_ a mistake
2 …. something interesting
3 …. friends
4 …. your homework
5 …. a phone call
6 …. the right thing

3 Write the material for each object.

1 _glass_

4 Complete the text with the words in the box.

> ~~consume~~   saves   leave   wastes
> reduce   switch off   turn down

People generally ¹ _consume_ a large amount of energy every day. There are a number of ways to ² …. your energy bills and help the environment at the same time. ³ …. your heating in the winter – wear an extra sweater instead! Using cold water to wash clothes also ⁴ …. energy. ⁵ …. appliances when you are not using them. Some people ⁶ …. their TV or computer on standby all night and that ⁷ …. a lot of electricity.

Explore vocabulary

5 Complete the text with the words in the box.

> ~~propose~~   vote   together   throw away
> shaped   match   decorations   reuse (x2)

Adam: We need to decide on the theme for the end-of-school party. What does everyone ¹ _propose_ ?
Bella: What about a ball with an eco theme?
Adam: Okay. What do you mean?
Bella: Well, we could ² …. coloured waste paper to make ³ …. .
Chris: That's a good idea – we ⁴ …. a lot of paper and it's a good way to ⁵ …. it.
Adam: Good, so who wants to make them?
Chris: Bella and I can do that ⁶ …. .
Bella: Could we have paper plates ⁷ …. like leaves?
Chris: How does that ⁸ …. the eco theme?
Bella: Trees – the environment …
Adam: Oh okay, yes. Right, let's ⁹ …. . Who's in favour of the eco-theme ball?
All: Yes!

6 Complete the text with the words in the box.

> ~~pick up~~   find out   write out   work out
> try out   keep on   put up   knock down
> cut down

1 George _picked up_ French really quickly when we went to Paris.
2 My dad …. a tree house for us in our garden when we were young.
3 I'm going to …. my new bike at the weekend.
4 A: I can't …. the answer to this Maths problem.
   B: I know it's difficult, but you should …. trying to find the answer.
5 We need to …. about renewable energy in our country for a school project.
6 They had to …. that beautiful old tree in our street – it was dangerous.
7 Can you …. your full name and address here, please?
8 Did you know that they are going to …. that building? It's old and dangerous.

Language focus

1 Complete the sentences with the verbs in brackets. Use the second conditional.
1. If you *were* (be) more confident, you *would make* (make) more friends.
2. If he …. (not go) to school, he …. (be) bored.
3. If they …. (wear) uniforms, they …. (look) the same.
4. We …. (have) more free time if we …. (not have) so much homework.
5. You …. (not be) so tired if you …. (not stay) up late.
6. If she …. (study) harder, she …. (get) better marks at school.

2 Write questions using the second conditional.
1. What / you / do / if / you / see someone cheating in a test?
   What would you do if you saw someone cheating in a test?
2. Where / you / live / if / you / can go anywhere in the world?
3. If / you / win / 5,000 euros / what / you / do?
4. If / your friend / not answer / your email / what / you / say?
5. If / you / not pass / your next test / you / feel upset?

3 Write sentences using the present simple passive.
1. They recycle these metal tins. *These metal tins are recycled.*
2. They make these sweaters from plastic bottles.
3. They use corn to make heating oil.
4. They produce electricity from this water.
5. They build these houses from organic materials.
6. Solar energy heats the water.

4 Complete the sentences with the past passive of the verbs in the box. Then write a question for each statement.

| discover | build | ~~make~~ | destroy | grow | not eat |

1. The first talking film *was made* in 1927.
   When *was the first talking film made*?
2. Tea …. in China 4,000 years ago.
   When …. in China?
3. Gold …. in California in the 19th century.
   Where …. in the 19th century?
4. Pompeii …. by a volcanic eruption in 79AD.
   When …. by a volcanic eruption?
5. Tomatoes …. in Europe until the 16th century.
   When …. in Europe?
6. The first public railways …. in England in the 19th century.
   Where …. ?

Language builder

UNIT 7–8

5 Choose the correct words to complete the conversation.

Tom: If you [1] *a* your own blog on the Internet, what [2] …. about?

Hanna: About the environment. Lots of blogs about the environment [3] …. on the Internet, but not many of them [4] …. for teenagers. I want to help the planet. If we [5] …. something now, then it [6] …. too late.

Tom: I agree. I read about a music blog. It [7] …. by a teenager a couple of years ago. It [8] …. by thousands of people and later he became a music journalist.

Hanna: So if my blog [9] …. popular, then someone [10] …. me a job as a journalist, too!

Tom: Who knows? I think I [11] …. a blog. Let's write it together.

	a	b	c
1	wrote	would write	will write
2	will it be	would it be	is it
3	published	are published	publish
4	are written	are writing	are write
5	are not doing	not do	don't do
6	is	would be	will be
7	started	was starting	was started
8	read	was reading	was read
9	becomes	is becoming	would become
10	will probably give	gives probably	probably is giving
11	started	might start	am starting

Speaking

6 Match the sentences.
1. I need your advice. *b*
2. What do you think I should do?
3. I'm really sorry.
4. I sent you a text to remind you!
5. Have you tried talking to him?
6. Oh well, how about next week?

a. If I were you, I wouldn't listen to him.
b. What's the problem?
c. Yes, I know. I really meant to come, honest!
d. No, I haven't – that's a good idea.
e. Okay, never mind.
f. Yes, great, I'll come.

Say it right!

Unit 5 Intonation in first conditional sentences

1 🔊 2.08 **Listen and repeat.**

1 If you speak good English, you'll get a better job.
2 I'll go to university if I pass my exams.

2 🔊 2.09 **Listen and mark the fall-rising (↗) and falling (↘) intonation on the stressed words in the sentences.**

1 If he doesn't call, I'll send him a message.
2 You'll meet my friends if you get there early.
3 If you don't listen to me, you won't understand.
4 I'll make more friends in London if I speak good English.
5 He'll help if we have a problem.
6 If we get homework, I won't go out.

3 🔊 2.09 **Listen, check and repeat.**

4 Practise saying the sentences in Exercise 2 with the correct intonation.

Unit 6 ough

1 🔊 2.19 **Listen and repeat.**

> enough   through   thought   although

2 🔊 2.20 **Listen and choose the correct sound.**

1 I think that's enough.	/ʌ/	/uː/
2 We walked through the park.	/ʌ/	/oʊ/
3 I thought it was scary.	/ɔː/	/uː/
4 Although I like her, she's not my best friend.	/ʌ/	/oʊ/
5 I bought a new T-shirt yesterday.	/ɔː/	/uː/
6 Even though I'm afraid of insects, I like butterflies.	/ʌ/	/oʊ/

3 🔊 2.20 **Listen, check and repeat.**

Unit 7 Intonation in second conditional sentences

1 🔊 2.26 **Listen and repeat.**

1 If I was rude to the teacher, I'd get detention.
2 I'd study Art if I went to a Free school.

2 🔊 2.27 **Listen and mark the fall-rising (↗) and falling (↘) intonation on the stressed words in the sentences.**

1 If I was headteacher of my school, I would make the lunch breaks longer.
2 If you lived in the UK, your life would be different.
3 I wouldn't give any homework if I was a teacher.
4 I'd go to the cinema if it was my birthday tomorrow.

3 🔊 2.27 **Listen, check and repeat.**

4 Practise saying the sentences in Exercise 2 with the correct intonation.

Unit 8 Stress in compound words

1 🔊 2.35 **Listen and repeat.**

> metal cans   glass bottle   car tyre
> earthquake   cotton T-shirt   solar energy

2 Mark the stress on the compound words.

> birthday cake   sun cream   leather shoes
> paper plates   sun hat   sweet wrappers
> plastic glasses   brick wall
> swimming pool   plastic table

3 🔊 2.36 **Listen, check and repeat.**

Grammar reference

Unit 5

will, might/may

+	I/He/She/It/We/You/They	might/may	help.
–		might not/may not	
?	Might/May	I/he/she/it/we/you/they	help?
+	Yes,	I/he/she/it/we/you/they	might/may.
–	No,		might not/may not.

- We can use *will* and *might/may* to give our opinions about the future.
  When she gets here, she'll want to speak to you.
  I might travel round the world next year.
  She may go to India next year.
- We use *will* and *won't* to show we are sure about the future.
  We'll go to the party later.
  She won't text you because she's angry with you.
- We use *might/may* and *might not/may not* to show we are not sure about the future.
  I might go to the party later. (I'm not sure.)
  She may not call you if she's busy.
- We use an infinitive without *to* after *will* and *might/may*.
  He'll to go shopping.   He may to go out later.

1 Complete the conversations with might (not)/ may (not) or will and the ideas in brackets.

1. A: What are you doing this weekend?
   B: I'm not sure. I *might stay in* . (stay in)
2. A: Where are you going to meet Megan?
   B: We haven't decided. We ..... (at the park)
3. A: I hope she gets the tickets.
   B: Relax. The stadium is really big – the tickets ..... (not sell out)
4. A: I've bought Harry a birthday present.
   B: I'm sure he ..... (love it)
5. A: When is Paula going to see Ethan?
   B: I think ..... (on Thursday)

Adverbs of possibility

- We often use adverbs after *will* and *might* to emphasise our feelings about the future.
- We often use *definitely* and *certainly* with *will* to emphasise we are sure about a future event or action.
  I'll definitely have a look at the website this evening.
  They certainly won't win the match against Liverpool.
- We often use *probably* with *will* to emphasise we are not completely sure about a future action or event.
  Natalie will probably be interested in this.

2 Choose the correct words.

1. I'll (probably) / certainly buy the red one, but I'm going to think about it.
2. She'll definitely / probably be late. She always is!
3. We definitely will / 'll definitely do it.
4. They will probably / certainly will need some help.
5. He probably / definitely won't know, but ask!
6. Computers will certainly / definitely will take over the world – the question is when!

First conditional + may/might, be able to

	Situation	Consequence
+	If I pass all my exams,	my parents might buy me a present.
–	If I don't pass all my exams,	my parents won't buy me a present.
	Consequence	Situation
–	My parents may not buy me a present	if I don't pass all my exams.
?	Will my parents buy me a present	if I pass all my exams?

- We use the first conditional to talk about possible situations in the present or future and say what we think the result will be.
- We often use *if* and the present simple to describe the possible action or event.
  If he doesn't email me, I won't speak to him again.
- We use *will/won't* + infinitive when we are sure of the result.
  If we don't leave now, we won't catch the 8.30 bus.
- We use *may/might (not)* to show we are less sure about the consequence.
  If she sees you, she might leave.
- We use *be able to* to talk about possible abilities.
  I'll be able to buy it if I save the money.
- When we use *if* to start the sentence, we use a comma between the two parts.
  If I see him, I'll give him the present.
  I'll give him the present if I see him

3 Complete the sentences with the correct form of the verb phrases in the box.

> not listen careful   speak quietly   not remind them
> tell him to call me   ~~go to the park~~

1. If it's sunny tomorrow, we'*ll go to the park* .
2. If you see him, ... you .... ?
3. You won't understand if you ..... .
4. They might not do it if you ..... .
5. He won't be frightened if you ..... .

Grammar reference   103

Grammar reference

Unit 6

be going to/will/Present continuous

+	I	'm	
	He/She/It	's	
	We/You/They	're	
			tell him.
-	I	'm not	going to
	He/She/It	isn't	
	We/You/They	aren't	
?	Am	I	
	Is	he/she/it	tell him?
	Are	we/you/they	

- We use *be going to* to talk about future actions we intend to do.
  After we finish school, I'm going to go to work.
  My grandparents are going to stay with us at the weekend.
- We use *will* to talk about predictions in the future.
  She won't find it – she always gets lost!
  They'll be late for the party. They always are.
  *See unit 5 for how we form *will*.
- We use the present continuous to talk about future arrangements when they have a fixed date.
  They're getting married this summer.
  She isn't coming to the party.
  *See unit 1 for how we form the present continuous.

1 Choose the correct form to complete the conversation.

> A: What time ¹(are you catching)/ will you catch the bus to London?
> B: Eleven o'clock – so I ² will leave / 'm leaving in ten minutes. I ³ will / 'm going to meet Alex at the bus station.
> A: What ⁴ are you going to / will you do in London?
> B: Well, I think the weather ⁵ will be / is being nice so we ⁶ will / 're going to take a boat ride along the Thames. Then we've got tickets for a walking tour so we're ⁷ going to meet / meeting our guide at one o'clock in Trafalgar Square.
> A: That sounds like fun. Have a great time.

Quantifiers – *how much/many*, *(not) enough*, *too many/much*

	Countable (plural)	uncountable	both
+	a few	a little	(not) enough
-	too many	too much	(not) enough
?	too many	too much	(not) enough

- We use quantifiers to express the quantity of something.
- When the noun is countable we always use the plural form.
  My sister has got too many toys.
- We use *too + much/many* to say that an amount is excessive. The difference between *too much* and *too many* is the same as the difference between *much* and *many*. *Too much* is used with singular (uncountable) nouns; *too many* is used with plurals.
  There are too many books for one person to carry.
  They eat too much fast food.
- We use *how much/how many* to ask about quantity.
  How much money have you got?
  How many books are there?
- We use *enough* to say a quantity is sufficient and *not enough* to say a quantity is insufficient.
  I didn't have enough time to answer all the questions.
  We've got enough players to make two teams.

a little/a few

- We use *a little* and *a few* to express small quantities.
  I've got a few emails that I need to reply to.
  There's a little chocolate ice cream.
- Use *a few* with plural countable nouns.
  I've got a few questions about phobias.
- We use *a little* with uncountable nouns.
  Can I have a little sugar?

2 Complete the sentences with the words in the box.

> ~~too much~~   a few   enough
> how many   a little   too many

1 I had ...*too much*... coffee and now I can't sleep.
2 You've got .... sweets – put some back.
3 I don't think we have .... money for cake.
4 .... students are there in your class?
5 There's only .... milk left – should I buy some?
6 I've got .... things to do today.

Grammar reference

Unit 7

Second conditional – affirmative and negative

	Imaginary situation	Possible consequence
	(*if* + past simple)	(*would* + infinitive)
+	If you woke up earlier,	you would arrive on time.
-	If she didn't talk in class,	she wouldn't get detention.
	Consequence	Situation
	(*would* + infinitive)	(*if* + past simple)
+	You would arrive on time	if you woke up earlier.
-	She wouldn't get detention	if she didn't talk in class.

- We use second conditional sentences to talk about imaginary situations and the possible consequences. Both parts can be affirmative or negative.
  We'd be in Berlin now if we'd caught the early train.
  If he didn't go to work, he wouldn't be so tired.
- We use *if* + past simple (affirmative or negative) to describe the imaginary situation.
  If I didn't have a dog, I'd like to have a cat.
- We use *would* (*not*) + infinitive to express an imaginary result we are sure of. When *would* is affirmative, we usually contract it *'d*. The negative is usually *wouldn't*.
  If she didn't like you, she wouldn't send you texts.
  They'd get better grades if they studied.
- We can use *was* or *were* in the *if* part of the sentence with *I*, *he/she* and *it*.
  I'd be quiet and not say anything if I were/was you.
  If my sister wasn't/weren't at university, I'd still have to share a bedroom.
- When we use *if* to start the sentence, use a comma between the two parts.
  If I had more money, I'd buy a new mobile.

1 Match the sentence halves.

1 If he went to India,   _e_
2 She would love to see you   ....
3 There would be less pollution ....
4 If I was a teacher, ...
5 You wouldn't believe me   ....
6 If he joined the football team, ...

a if people didn't use their cars every day.
b he'd make lots of friends.
c if you had time to come.
d if I told you.
e he'd visit Bombay.
f I wouldn't give any homework.

2 Complete the second conditional sentences. Use the correct form of the verbs in brackets.

1 If I __had__ (have) time, I __'d learn__ (learn) to play the guitar.
2 She .... (not be) late for school if she .... (get up) earlier.
3 If they .... (know) the answer, they .... (tell) you.
4 Mr Jones .... (help) you if you .... (ask) him nicely.
5 If I .... (meet) Will Smith, I .... (ask) for his autograph.
6 Our English .... (get) better if we .... (move) to New York.

Second conditional – questions

Imaginary situation	Possible consequence
(*if* + past simple)	(*would* + infinitive)
If I helped you with your homework,	would you lend me your MP3 player?
Would your dad take us to the concert	if you asked him?

- We form questions using *if* + past simple, *would(n't)* + subject + verb.
  If I told you a secret, would you promise not to tell?
  If I didn't reply to your messages, wouldn't you get angry?
  Wouldn't life be better if we had a five-day weekend?

3 Complete the questions with *would* and the correct form of the verbs in the box.

catch   go   say   can   ~~have~~   need

1 If you __had__ a dog, what __would__ you call it?
2 If you didn't feel ill, where .... you .... today?
3 What time .... we arrive if we .... the earlier train?
4 If you .... be a character from a film, who .... you be?
5 If he asked you to go out, ... you .... yes?
6 Who .... you ask if you .... to borrow some money?

4 Write second conditional questions with the prompts.

1 we / share a bedroom / how often / we / argue?
   If we shared a bedroom, how often would we argue?
2 they / like / it / I / stop / speaking to them?
3 What / his parents / say / they / know?
4 you / can / have a super power / what / it / be?
5 you / live in England / come home / often?
6 you / be / me / what / you / do?

Grammar reference

Unit 8

Present simple passive

+	This bottle	is made	of plastic
	These toys	are made	
-	This bottle	isn't made	
	These toys	aren't made	
?	Is	this bottle	made	of plastic?
	Are	these toys		
Yes, it is/they are.		No, it isn't/they aren't.	

- We use the passive to describe a process. We are usually not interested in, or don't know, who does this process.
  English is spoken in most shops and restaurants.
  Credit cards aren't accepted with ID.
- To form the present simple passive we use *is/are* (*not*) + past participle.
  Coffee isn't grown in Europe.
  The streets are cleaned on Sundays.
  * See page 126 for a list of irregular past participles.
- We form questions with *is/are* + subject + past participle. We put *Wh-* question words before *is/are*.
  Is the main square decorated in the holidays?
  When are the exam results emailed to students?
  How many photos are uploaded a week?

1 Use a word from each box to complete the sentences. Use the present simple passive.

bananas spaghetti cakes		drink catch cook
~~tea~~ fish chocolate		bake make grow

1 *Tea is drunk* in most countries.
2 .... from cocoa beans.
3 .... in an oven.
4 .... in rivers and at sea.
5 .... in Jamaica.
6 .... in boiling water.

2 Rewrite the sentences using the present simple passive.

1 They clean the windows every month.
   The windows are cleaned every month.
2 They don't update their blog every day.
3 People take a lot of photos on mobile phones.
4 The hotel serves breakfast from 7–10 am.
5 Do they give students a certificate at the end of the year?
6 People ask a lot of questions in my class.

Past simple passive

+	The rubbish was	thrown away.
	The old chairs were	
-	The rubbish wasn't	
	The old chairs weren't	
?	Was the rubbish	thrown away?
	Were the old chairs	
Yes, it was/they were.	No, it wasn't/they weren't.

- We use the past simple passive to describe processes in the past.
  Last year, a trip to Italy was organised at the end of term.
  The competition winners were given books.
- To form the past simple passive we use *was/were* (*not*) + past participle.
  The first Disney film was made in 1937.
  Some of us weren't invited to the party.
- To form questions we use *was/were* + subject + past participle. We put *Wh-* question words before *was/were*.
  Were the instructions written in English?
  How much money was taken from her bag?
  In which country was the telephone invented?

Passive + *by*

- We use *by* with the passive to show who was responsible for the actions.
  A lot of houses were destroyed by the fire.
  Who was the song Tell me a lie *recorded by? I think it was (recorded by) One Direction.*

3 Complete the text with the past passive form of the verbs in brackets. Use *by* when necessary.

Modern text messages, or SMS, [1] *were invented* (invent) in 1992. Early messages [2] .... (not write) on a mobile phone, they could only be sent from a computer to a phone. In 1993, the first mobile-to-mobile SMS service [3] .... (introduce) in Sweden. It wasn't immediately popular, but by 2011, an average of 19.9 billion texts [4] .... (send) people every day. In the same year, SMS messages [5] .... (replace) chat apps, such as WhatsApp. They [6] .... (use) to send 19 billion texts a day. Experts think this number is going to double in the next two years.

Vocabulary Bank

Jog your memory!

1 Cover the rest of the page. How many communication words can you remember?

Communication (page 53)

blog post	phone call
chatting	Skype™
email	text message
social media post	Tweet
forum	

1 Look at the words in the box. Where can you …
- see pictures and information about your friends?
- see and talk to someone?
- only use 140 characters to say what you want?
- read about someone's thoughts, opinions or experiences?
- talk about a subject with other people online?

Communication verbs (page 56)

argue	gossip
boast	joke
complain	shout
criticise	whisper

1 Look at the words in the box. Write sentences about each verb.

I often argue with my sister.

2 Work with a partner. Read your sentences but don't say the verb. Your partner guesses the verb.

You should …. in the library. (whisper)

Explore communication collocations (page 54)

digital	friends
face-	generation
social	network sites
status	to-face
virtual	update

1 Look at the words in the boxes. Match them to make collocations.

digital generation

2 Look at the text on page 54. Can you complete three more collocations?
- a …. media
- b online ….
- c …. forum

Explore phrasal verbs (page 59)

go up
get by
keep on
come into use
turn into

1 Look at the phrasal verbs in the box. Work with a partner and write an example sentence for each one.

2 Check your answers on page 59. Correct any sentences that are wrong.

Study tip

Sort words in your vocabulary book by collocations.

Vocabulary Bank

🧠 Jog your memory!

1 Cover the rest of the page. How many words to describe fears and adjectives can you remember?

Fears (page 63)

| birds | flying | insects | snakes |
| clowns | heights | lifts | the dark |

1 Look at the words in the box. Write the fears in the correct column.

animals	people	things
birds		

2 Can you add three more fears to the list?

-ed and -ing adjectives (page 66)

bored / boring	excited / exciting
terrified / terrifying	tired / tiring
interested / interesting	worried / worrying

1 Look at the words in the box. Write six sentences. Use three *-ing* adjectives and three *-ed* adjectives.
That film was really boring. I'm terrified of spiders.

🔍 Explore prepositional phrases (page 64)

embarrassed ....
share something .... someone
terrified ....
think ....
worried ....

1 Look at the words in the box. Write the correct preposition (*of*, *about* or *with*) to make prepositional phrases.

2 Do these words go with *about* or *of*? Which two words match both *about* and *of*?

| afraid | talk | fear | think |
| nightmare | scared | phobia | excited |

3 Write four sentences about yourself.
I always get excited about parties.

🔍 Explore opposite adjectives (page 69)

bad	dangerous
modern	good
safe	lucky
sensible	old
unlucky	silly
unsuccessful	successful

1 Look at the words in boxes. Match the opposite adjectives.
bad/good

2 You can add *un-* to one more adjective to make it opposite. Which adjective is it? Can you think of any other adjectives that you can add the prefix *un-* to?

3 Choose four of the words. Write four sentences using the words.

unlucky, unsuccessful

📖 Study tip

Write prefixes in a different colour.

112 Vocabulary Bank

Vocabulary Bank

🌐 Jog your memory!

1 Cover the rest of the page. How many school words can you remember?

Life at school (page 75)

be	hand	wear	bullying	get
scream	write	cheat	get	

a uniform	in a test	on time
detention	in homework	or shout
good marks	lines	

1 Look at the words in the boxes. Match them to make phrases about life at school. There is one word which doesn't match anything. Which word is it?

2 Look back at page 75 and check your answers.

3 Talk to your partner. What happens in your school? Use the words in the box to discuss.

make and *do* (page 78)

a mess	a decision
a mistake	friends
a noise	something interesting
a phone call	the right thing
an exercise	your homework

1 Look at the words in the box. Match the words with the correct verbs.

make	do
a mess	

2 Look back at page 78 and check your answers.

3 Work with a partner. Test him/her. Close your books. Say a word. Your partner says the correct verb, *make* or *do*.

🔍 Explore phrasal verbs (page 81)

find out	work out	try out
pick up	write out	

1 Look at the definitions on page 81 again. Write a sentence with each phrasal verb that is personal to you and shows its meaning.
I like finding out about other countries.
It's interesting.

2 Look at these phrasal verbs with *out* and *up*. Discuss their meaning with a partner. Use a dictionary to help you.

log out	go out	look up
drop out	grow up	hang up

📖 Study tip

Listen to music and watch films to help you learn new vocabulary. Remember to write new words in your vocabulary notebook.

Vocabulary Bank

🧠 Jog your memory!

1 Cover the rest of the page. How many words to describe materials and energy issues can you remember?

Materials (page 85)

bricks	metal
cement	paper
cotton	plastic
glass	rubber
leather	wood

1 Look at the words in the box. Think about your house. Write an object you can find there for each type of material in the box.
bricks – my garden wall

2 Work with a partner. Take turns to read your descriptions and guess the material.
A: My favourite T-shirt!   B: Cotton?

Energy issues (page 88)

consume
leave on standby
reduce
save energy
switch off
turn down
waste

1 Turn to page 88. Look at the definitions again.

2 Can you remember them all? Give examples of what you do to save energy in your house.
I never leave the TV on standby.

🔍 Explore phrasal verbs (page 91)

bring	*down*	knock	....
cut	....	put	....
keep	....		

1 Look at the verbs in the box. Write *down*, *on* or *up* to make a phrasal verb.

2 Check your answers on page 91. Can you think of an example sentence for each phrasal verb?
When they brought down the price of the laptop, I had enough money to buy it.

consume (verb) [T]
/kənˈsjuːm/
to use fuel, energy or time, especially in large amounts

📅 Study tip

Use a dictionary to check how words are spelt, the pronunciation and the type of word it is.

5 CLIL

Technology Early written communication

1 Work with a partner Answer the questions.
- When did people start writing?
- How did the ancient Egyptians write?
- Where does the word 'alphabet' come from?

2 🔊 2.44 Read the text and check your ideas.

Our earliest human ancestors first stood on two legs around 6 million years ago. But it was the ability to share information which set our ancestors apart from the rest of the animals. Communication remained very limited until our closest ancestor, Homo erectus, appeared about 1.8 million years ago. But it was only 6,000 years ago, with Homo sapiens, that any form of writing came into existence.

The earliest forms of writing were logographic and used symbols (logograms) to represent things. The most famous of these old forms of writing is hieroglyphics. The Ancient Egyptians either carved or painted hieroglyphs on stone. However, they also had two other forms of writing, called hieratic and demotic. They wrote onto papyrus, a form of paper, or cloth with ink or paint. We know a lot about hieroglyphic writing because of the Rosetta Stone. This is an ancient stone slab with the same message written in hieroglyphics, demotic and Ancient Greek.

Alphabetic writing systems use marks which represent sounds. Ancient Greek was the first complete alphabet and represented both consonant and vowel sounds. In fact, the word alphabet comes from the first two Greek letters, alpha and beta. It was a unique invention and many different languages now use some form of complete alphabet. English uses the Roman alphabet, which the Romans adapted from the ancient Greek.

3 Read the text again. Are the sentences true or false? Correct the false ones.
1. Homo erectus used a logographic writing system.
2. The ancient Egyptians had three forms of writing.
3. The Egyptians carved hieroglyphs into stone.
4. The Ancient Greek alphabet only represented consonant sounds.
5. The Romans adapted their alphabet from hieroglyphics.

4 Complete the text with the words in the box.

> logograms x2   spoken   alphabets
> logographic   alphabetic   pronunciation

Hieroglyphics was a [1].... system of writing. It used [2].... to represent objects and actions. Because they were not related to [3]...., different languages could use the same [4].....
[5].... systems of writing use marks to represent sounds of the [6].... language so different languages might use the same [7].... but spelling and grammar will be different.

5 🔊 2.45 Listen to a linguist talking about reading and writing. What subjects does he talk about?
a The Romans
b dangerous animals
c books for wealthy people
d cheap books
e Internet blogs

Your turn

6 Work with a partner and write a short message. Write the message using only pictures. Show your message to the rest of the class to see if they can work it out.

Learn about hieroglyphics.
- What has the archaeologist come to see?
- How long has the skeleton been there?
- Why was the sandal strap important to Egyptians?

Discovery EDUCATION

5.4 Pictures with meaning

6 CLIL

Geography Living in a global city

1 Work with a partner. Look at the photos. Which cities are they? Make a list of the advantages of living in a city.

2 🔊 2.46 Read the information about cities. Are any of your ideas from Exercise 1 mentioned?

3 Read the information again and complete the following summary.

> The economies of most cities are based on ¹*manufacturing* and ².... Services include public administration, health care, ³.... and ⁴....
> Global cities are important world ⁵.... centres. They have large ⁶.... populations. ⁷.... have their headquarters there. They are cultural centres with ⁸...., art galleries and ⁹....

4 🔊 2.47 Listen and check.

Your turn

5 Work with a partner. One of you look at Photo 1, the other at Photo 2. Make a list of the advantages of living in this place.

A city is a large, densely populated area with a high concentration of buildings and an infrastructure of services and facilities. Unlike rural areas, the majority of economic activities in cities is in manufacturing or services, like public administration, transport, health care and entertainment.

Cities can be classified in different ways. We can call them global, governmental, industrial or tourist, according to their main activity. Global cities usually combine aspects of all types, but their main importance is in the global economy.

As well as being important world economic centres, most global cities share various features. They usually have large cosmopolitan populations; they have the headquarters of multinational companies and they have cultural centres with important museums, art galleries and universities. Global cities usually have advanced public transport systems and a major airport. In general, global cities have an active influence on world events.

6 Discuss the advantages and disadvantages of living in the place in your photo.

Learn about Russian cities.
- What advantages are there for living in the countryside?
- How many people live in Moscow?
- What are people proud of in St Petersburg?

Discovery EDUCATION

6.4 City or country?

7 CLIL

Technology   Social media

1 Work with a partner. Answer the questions.
1. What social media sites do you use?
2. In what ways can social media be useful for teenagers?

2 🔊 2.48 Read the information about teenagers and social media. Check your ideas from Exercise 1.

Using social media can be a good thing.

Social media sites and networking can:

- improve communication between teenagers and their teachers, because they are available at all times from almost anywhere.
- encourage teenagers to interact with each other, share ideas and be creative by letting people communicate in different ways.
- help develop relationships with real people. They can help shy teenagers find friends who follow the same singers, sports stars and so on, and feel part of a group.
- expose teenagers to different viewpoints and new ideas through a wide variety of online communities.
- help teenagers get better at analysing and selecting important information. There's a lot of information on social media pages, so users become good at finding key information quickly.
- help familiarise students with new technologies. Social media sites are constantly changing – to stay up to date, teenagers have to learn new ways of using them.
- help students enter the world of work. Professional networking sites like LinkedIn™ can help people find out about different professions and job offers.

3 Read the text again. Which three benefits do you think are the most important? Compare with a partner.

4 🔊 2.49 Listen to three teenagers on a radio phone-in. Match the speakers to the social media they talk about.

John
Sarah
Mark

a can organise images and create collections on Pinterest
b likes Myspace because it's good for sharing music.
c uses Facebook to exchange messages and photos.
d likes Twitter because messages are short.

Your turn

5 Ask and answer with your partner.
1. What's your favourite social media site?
2. What do you like about it?
3. Is there anything you don't like about it?

Learn about being safe online.
- How can you be sure who you are talking to online?
- What does a criminal need to get a credit card?
- What should you do with messages from people you don't know?

Discovery EDUCATION

7.4 Be safe online

8 CLIL

Chemistry Renewable energy

1 Work with a partner. Look at the photos. How many sources of renewable energy can you think of?

2 🔊 **2.50** Read the information about sources of energy. Check your answers from Exercise 1.

At the moment we get about 70% of our energy from fossil fuels like oil, coal and natural gas, but there are two main problems with this. Firstly, they release CO_2 when we burn them and secondly, they take millions of years to form and the supply is limited.

Fossil fuels are not the only sources of energy. Alternative energy is energy generated from any source other than 'traditional' fossil fuels and which doesn't damage our environment. The sun (solar energy), wind (eolic energy), water (hydroelectric energy) and tides and waves (tidal and wave power) are all alternative energy sources. They are also called renewable energy because they won't run out or sustainable energy because we can use it now without affecting the supply in the future.

There are other sources of energy such as biofuel and nuclear power, but these are not strictly alternative energy sources. Biofuel is a term that includes a wide variety of fuels obtained from biomass (carbon-based biological material, usually plants), so it releases CO_2 in the same way as fossil fuels. Nuclear power doesn't produce CO_2, but it does produce waste which can stay toxic for 240,000 years.

Climate change and global warming, together with high oil prices and the risk of nuclear contamination, are making renewable energy sources more attractive. The production of alternative energy is growing very rapidly. It is estimated that 16% of all energy now comes from renewable resources.

3 Read the text again. Match the words in the box with the definitions.

> sustainable energy   renewable energy
> alternative energy   fossil fuels   biofuel

1 …. comes from sources that do not damage the environment.
2 …. comes from sources that do not run out.
3 …. gives us energy without affecting the supply in the future.
4 …. comes from material like plants.
5 …. are formed over millions of years from the remains of plants and animals.

4 Work with a partner. Answer the quiz questions about energy sources.

1 How much of the energy used by TVs is used while they're on standby?
  A 10%   C 60%
  B 35%   D 85%

2 How long can a game console run for if you recycle one aluminium can?
  A 30 minutes   C 2 hours
  B 1 hour   D 10 hours

3 Biodiesel is a kind of biofuel used in diesel engines. Which of these things CAN'T it be made from?
  A coconuts   C potatoes
  B used cooking oil D sunflower seeds

4 How much of the world's electricity does the Sun provide every 15 minutes?
  A Enough for three years.   C Enough for a day.
  B Enough for a year.   D Enough for a month.

5 🔊 **2.51** Listen and check.

Your turn

6 Work with a partner. Make a poster to encourage students in your school to recycle and save energy. Follow the steps below.
- Decide together what information to put on your poster.
- Find photos and pictures to illustrate the information.
- Present your poster to your class.
- Vote on the class's favourite poster.

Learn about electric cars.
- Which countries are producing electric cars?
- What is Kevin's goal?
- Where are car batteries made?

Discovery EDUCATION

8.4 Driving into the future

Project 3

An information leaflet

GREEN JEWELLERY

1 ....
This is a piece of recycled jewellery that your friends won't have. It is called a necklace and you wear it round your neck. It comes in different sizes and colours so you can pick your favourite one.

2 ....
Lego is a company that makes small, plastic building blocks for children. They put the pieces together to make cars, aeroplanes, houses and cities. Well, this necklace was made with plastic Lego pieces. In the past they were used for making Lego houses, boats, planes and castles. Now you can wear them on your body as jewellery like earrings, necklaces and bracelets.

3 ....
Jewellery is usually made from metal that is mined from the earth and this damages the environment. However, this jewellery is made with plastic from children's old toys. Plastic has a long life so if you don't reuse it, it will stay on a rubbish dump for the next four hundred years!

4 ....
You don't have to spend money to be fashionable. Why not try to make some jewellery at home? Use old toys, household objects and some elastic. Be creative and you can make your own designs for much less money.

Look

1 Match the words in the box with the pictures.

> bracelet   earring   jewellery   necklace

2 Read the text. Match the questions with the paragraphs.
   a   What can you make?
   b   What is it made of?
   c   Why is it the best 'green' product?
   d   What is it?

Prepare

3 Work in groups of three or four. Use the Internet to find examples of recycled products based on things you can find in your home. Choose your favourite one and make notes about it. Use the questions in Exercise 2 to help you.

4 Make an information leaflet on your favourite recycled product. Use photos or draw a picture of the product and the information in Exercise 3. Then think of a title which relates to the product and its use.

Present

5 Display the leaflet on the wall in your classroom. Ask your classmates to read it. Then test their memory using the questions in Exercise 2. Have a class vote to choose the best 'green' product.

Thanks and acknowledgements

The authors and publishers would like to thank all the teachers and consultants who have contributed to the development of this course, in particular:

Argentina: Fernando Armesto; Natalia Bitar; Verónica Borrás; Leonor Corradi ; Paz Moltrasio; Diana Ogando; Brazil: Dalmo Carvalho; Roberto Costa; Sônia M. B. Leites; Gloria Paz; Litany Pires Ribeiro; Christina Riego; Renata Condi de Souza; Elizabeth White; Chile: Magdalena Aldunate; M. Cristina Darraidou Diaz; Valentina Donoso; Ana María Páez Jofrré; Ricardo Contreras Marambio; Claudia Ottone; Maria Elena Ramirez; Jacqueline Rondon; Alicia Paez Ubilla; Colombia: Luz Amparo Bautista; Sonia Ruiz Hernández; Sandra Jara; Fabian Jimenez; Bibiana Andrea Piñeros Merizalde; Lucero Amparo Bernal Nieto; Olga Olarte; Bibiana Piñeros; Emelis Rambut; Sonia Ruíz; Poland: Anna Bylicka; Russia: Natalya Melchenkova; Irina Polyakova; Svetlana Suchkova; Irina Vayserberg; Turkey: Ali Bilgin; Angela Çakır; Shirley Nuttal; Cinla Sezgin; Mujgan Yesiloglu

The publishers are grateful to the following for permission to reproduce copyright photographs and material:
Cover: Alamy/©Martin Strimska; Back cover: Shutterstock Images/fluke samed; p. 6 (BR): Shutterstock Images/Prometheus72; p. 6 (TL): Alamy/©Stockbroker; p. 7 (TL): Shutterstock Images/Jacek Chabraszewski; p. 7 (TC): Shutterstock Images/scyther5; p. 7 (BC): Shutterstock Images/Ervin Monn; p. 8 (B/G): Getty Images/Stone; p. 9 (a): Shutterstock Images/Tom Wang; p. 9 (b): Shutterstock Images/fluke samed; p. 9 (c): Alamy/©blickwinkel; p. 9 (d): Alamy/©David R. Frazier Photolibrary Inc.; p. 9 (e): Shutterstock Images/egd; p. 9 (f): Shutterstock Images/Richard Whitcombe; p. 9 (g): Shutterstock Images/Igumnova Irina; p. 9 (h): Shutterstock Images/James BO Insogna; p. 10 (B): Alamy/©RIA Novosti; p. 10 (BC): Alamy/©RIA Novosti; p. 11 (TR): Alamy/©Kumar Sriskandan; p. 12-13 (B/G): Alamy/©Paul Mayall Australia; p. 14 (B/G T): Alamy/©Plinthpics; p. 14 (BR): Alamy/©Ben Pipe; p. 14 (C): Alamy/©Images of Africa Photobank; p. 14 (TR): Alamy/©Trish Ainslie; p. 14-15 (B/G): Alamy/©Chris Howarth/South Atlantic; p. 16 (TR): Alamy/©Ellen Isaacs; p. 16 (BR): Alamy/© VIEW Pictures Ltd/; p. 17 (TR): Alamy/©Tim Graham; p. 17 (BR): Shutterstock Images/Burro; p. 18 (B/G): Corbis/2/Arctic-Images/Ocean; p. 19 (a): Alamy/©Tetra Images; p. 19 (b): Alamy/©Kuttig - People; p. 19 (c): Alamy/©Justin Kase zsixz; p. 19 (d): Shutterstock Images/Masson; p. 19 (e): Shutterstock Images/kuznetcov_konstantin; p. 19 (f): Superstock/age footstock; p. 19 (g): Getty Images/Image Source; p. 19 (h): REX/Phanie/Garo; p. 20 (T): Getty Images/Susanne Walstrom/Johner Images; p. 22 (TR): Shutterstock Images/bullet74; p. 22 (BR): Alamy/©The Art Archive; p. 23 (BC): Shutterstock Images/Helder Almeida; p. 24 (T): Alamy/©Paul Doyle; p. 24 (CR): Alamy/©ZUMA Press Inc.; p. 25 (B/G): Alamy/©Ulrich Doering; p. 25 (BL): Alamy/©LondonPhotos - Homer Sykes; p. 26 (BL): Alamy/©Kumar Sriskandan; p. 26 (CR): Alamy/©Blend Images; p. 27 (TL): Getty Images/Cavan Images/Taxi; p. 27 (TC): Getty Images/Steve Mason/Photodisc; p. 27 (CL): Shutterstock Images/Anna Jurkovska; p. 30 (B/G): Alamy/©Nikreates; p. 31 (a): Alamy/©Ian Francis; p. 31 (b): Alamy/©Arco Images GmbH; p. 31 (c): Alamy/©JOHN KELLERMAN; p. 31 (d): Alamy/©Andrew Aitchison; p. 31 (e): Corbis/ Sylvain Sonnet; p. 31 (f): Alamy/©eddie linssen; p. 31 (g): Alamy/©Ferenc Szelepcsenyi; p. 31 (h): Getty Images/Getty Images Sport/Andy Lyons; p. 31 (i): Alamy/©Michele and Tom Grimm; p. 31 (j): Alamy/©Artepics; p. 32 (BL): Alamy/©LOOK Die Bildagentur der Fotografen GmbH; p. 33 (TR): Corbis/ Bernd Kammerer/dpa; p. 33 (BL): Getty Images/Maartje Van Caspel; p. 34 (1): Shutterstock Images/Andrey_Popov; p. 34 (2): Shutterstock Images/mphot; p. 34 (3): Shutterstock Images/Vereshchagin Dmitry; p. 34 (4): Shutterstock Images/Redkaya; p. 34 (5): Shutterstock Images/Furtseff; p. 34 (6): Shutterstock Images/vvoe; p. 34 (7): Shutterstock Images/grigiomedio; p. 34 (8): Shutterstock Images/J. Helgason; p. 34 (9): Shutterstock Images/Dario Sabljak; p. 34 (10): Shutterstock Images/Chromakey; p. 34 (11): Shutterstock Images/Visun Khankasem; p. 34 (12): Shutterstock Images/Mike Braune; p. 34 (13): Shutterstock Images/Jouke van Keulen; p. 34 (14): Alamy/©Aki; p. 34 (TR): Alamy/©i stage; p. 36 (a): Alamy/©Richard Ellis; p. 36 (b): Alamy/©Stephen Chung; p. 36 (c): Alamy/©Universal Images Group Limited; p. 37 (C): REX/KeystoneUSA-ZUMA; p. 37 (CR): Getty Images/r e y . t o r r e s/Moment Open; p. 37 (BR): Alamy/©ZUMA Press, Inc.; p. 38 (CL): Corbis/Dirk Lindner; p. 39 (TC): Alamy/©Gari Wyn Williams; p. 39 (TL): Alamy/©david pearson; p. 40 (B/G): Alamy/©Michael Jones/Alaska Stock; p. 41 (a): ©CUP/Mark Bassett; p. 41 (b): Alamy/©AugustSnow; p. 41 (c): Alamy/©Dmitry Burlakov; p. 41 (d): Getty Images/Ken Chernus/Taxi; p. 41 (e): Shutterstock Images/PhotoSky; p. 41 (f): Alamy/©ZUMA Press, Inc.; p. 41 (g): Shutterstock Images/wavebreakmedia; p. 41 (h): Shutterstock Images/Johnny Adolphson; p. 41 (i): Shutterstock Images/ Stephen B. Goodwin; p. 42 (BC): Alamy/©ianmurray; p. 42 (BR): Alamy/©Mar Photographics; p. 44 (TL): Alamy/©Alibi Productions; p. 45 (CR): Alamy/©Purepix; p. 46 (TR): Shutterstock Images/Lev Kropotov; p. 46 (TC): Alamy/©Howard Davies; p. 46 (B/G): Shutterstock Images/Tooykrub; p. 47 (BR): Alamy/©Blaine Harrington III; p. 47 (TR): Alamy/©Allstar Picture Library; p. 47 (TC): Agefotostock/Stuart Blac; p. 48 (TL): Alamy/©Hemis; p. 48 (CR): Shutterstock Images/Strahil Dimitrov; p. 48 (BR): Alamy/©PhotoAlto; p. 49 (TR): Alamy/©Jochen Tack; p. 49 (TL): Alamy/©Wim Wiskerke; p. 50 (BR): Shutterstock Images/Gigi Peis; p. 51 (CR): Shutterstock Images/S.Borisov; p. 52 (B/G): Getty Images/Riou; p. 53 (a): Alamy/©Catchlight Visual Services; p. 53 (b): Alamy/©Buzzshotz; p. 53 (c): Alamy/©Anatolii Babii; p. 53 (d): Alamy/©IanDagnall Computing; p. 53 (e): Alamy/©NetPhotos; p. 53 (f): Alamy/©pumkinpie; p. 54-55 (b): Alamy/©Eric Audras; p. 56 (a): Shutterstock Images/Goran Djukanovic; p. 56 (b): Alamy/©John Powell/ Bubbles Photolibrary; p. 56 (c): Shutterstock Images/Tomasz Trojanowski; p. 56 (d): Alamy/©Blend Images; p. 57 (C): Alamy/©eye35.pix; p. 58 (T): Alamy/©Iain Masterton; p. 58 (CL): Alamy/©AKP Photos; p. 59 (BL): Alamy/©Top Photo/Asia Photo Connection/Henry Westheim Photography; p. 59 (BR): Shutterstock Images/Elena Elisseeva; p. 59 (TL): Alamy/©Bazza; p. 59 (BC): Alamy/©Liquid Light; p. 60 (TL): Alamy/©Valerie Garner; p. 60 (BL): Shutterstock Images/Deborah Kolb; p. 61 (TL): Shutterstock Images/Alexey Boldin; p. 62 (B/G): Getty Images/Jay P. Morgan; p. 63 (B/G): Shutterstock Images/Salajean; p. 63 (a): Alamy/©Robin Beckham/BEEPstock; p. 63 (b): Shutterstock Images/Jayakumar; p. 63 (c): Shutterstock Images/Dmitrijs Bindemanis; p. 63 (d): Shutterstock Images/Matteo photos; p. 63 (e): Shutterstock Images/Lisa F. Young; p. 63 (f): Shutterstock Images/Jag_cz; p. 64 (BC): Shutterstock Images/Sarah2; p. 64 (TC): Alamy/©Radius Images; p. 64 (C): Shutterstock Images/juniart; p. 64 (B): Alamy/©Image Source; p. 65 (BL): /Shutterstock Images/Sergei A. Aleshi; p. 66 (L): Alamy/©Gunter Marx; p. 66 (C): Getty Images/Petri Artturi Asikainen/Folio Images; p. 66 (R): Superstock/Greer & Associates, Inc.; p. 67 (TL): Alamy/©Ruby; p. 68 (TR): Alamy/©Peter Horree; p. 68 (BL): Alamy/©Tuul/Robert Harding World Imagery; p. 68 (B/G): Alamy/©Dbimages; p. 69 (BL): Alamy/©Adrian Turner; p. 69 (CR): Alamy/©David Gee; p. 69 (CL): Shutterstock Images/Sergio Foto; p. 69 (TR): Alamy/©Photodreams1; p. 69 (TL): Alamy/©Felipe Rodriguez; p. 69 (BR): Shutterstock Images/Olga Selyutina; p. 69 (CT):

Shutterstock Images/ Erni; p. 70 (CL): Alamy/©James Nesterwitz; p. 70 (CR): Getty Images/Echo/ultura; p. 70 (BR): Superstock/Marka; p. 71 (T): Getty Images/Elisabeth Schmitt/Moment Select; p. 72 (CR): Alamy/©Blue Jean Images; p. 73(TR): Shutterstock Images/cvrestan; p. 74 (B/G): Alamy/©Jennifer Podis/The Palm Beach Post/Zuma press; p. 75 (a): Alamy/©RubberBall; p. 75 (b): Alamy/©Westend61 GmbH; p. 75 (c): Corbis/©David Lefranc; p. 75 (d): Alamy/©imageBROKER; p. 75 (e): Shutterstock Images/BKMCphotography; p. 75 (f): Superstock/Image Source; p. 75 (g): Alamy/©Beyond Fotomedia GmbH; p. 75 (i): Getty Images/Silvia Otte/Taxi; p. 75 (f): Superstock/Image Source; p. 75 (h): Alamy/©Wavebreakmedia Ltd UC1; p. 76-77 (B): Alamy/©Riedmiller; p. 79 (CR): Alamy/©kt spencer march; p. 80 (TR): Getty Images/Inti St Clair/Digital Vision; p. 80 (TL): Alamy/©Ian Shaw; p. 80 (CR): Alamy/©Gregg Vignal; p. 81 (B/G): Shutterstock Images/oksana.perkins; p. 82 (TR): Alamy/©Image Source; p. 82 (CR): Alamy/©Tony Cordoza; p. 82 (BR): Alamy/©Marjorie Kamys Cotera/Bob Daemmrich Photography; p. 84 (B/G): Shutterstock Images/majeczka; p. 85 (a): Alamy/©imageBROKER; p. 85 (b): Alamy/©Steffen Hauser/botanikfoto; p. 85 (c): Q2A Media; p. 85 (d): Shutterstock Images/Sakarin Sawasdinaka; p. 85 (e): Q2A Media; p. 85 (f): Alamy/©Tom Merton/OJO Images Ltd; p. 85 (g): Q2A Media; p. 85 (h): Shutterstock Images/Kati Molin; p. 85 (i): Shutterstock Images/graphyx; p. 85 (j): Alamy/©Milena Boniek; p. 86 (CL): Alamy/©ZUMA Press; p. 86 (BL): Alamy/©Jay Goebel; p. 86-87 (B): Rex Features/Paul Cooper; p. 87 (TR): Corbis/Kirsten Neumann/Reuters; p. 88 (TL): Alamy/©Bubbles Photolibrary; p. 89 (B): Shutterstock Images/ Subbotina Anna; p. 90 (TL): Alamy/©US Labor Department; p. 90 (BL): Alamy/©Craig Ruttle; p. 90 (T): Getty Images/ Willoughby Owen; p. 91(CR): Shutterstock Images/Tchara; p. 91 (BR): Shutterstock Images/Daniel Schweinert; p. 91 (TR): Alamy/©Clynt Garnham Renewable Energy; p. 92 (BL): Superstock/imageBROKER; p. 92 (CR): Getty Images/Karl Lehmann/Lonely Planet Images; p. 92 (BR): Shutterstock Images/spwidoff; p. 93 (T): Alamy/©Todd Bannor; p. 93 (TR): Alamy/©Dave Porter; p. 95 (TR): Getty Images/Chris Schmidt; p. 107 (TR): Alamy/©Alaska Stock; p. 108 (TL): REX/Garo/ Phanie; p. 108 (TR): Shutterstock Images/Masson; p. 108 (BR): Alamy/©Ted Foxx; p. 108 (BL): Alamy/©Blend Images; p. 109 (TR): Alamy/©Arco Images GmbH; p. 109 (BL): Alamy/©eddie linssen; p. 109 (TL): Alamy/©Alex Segre; p. 109 (BR): Shutterstock Images/koi88; p. 110 (TC): Getty Images/Ken Chernus; p. 110 (TR): Shutterstock Images/Stephen B. Goodwin; p. 110 (C): Shutterstock Images/Johnny Adolphson; p. 110 (BR): Alamy/©Juice Images; p. 111 (TR): Getty Images/Silvia Otte/Taxi; p. 111 (TL): Alamy/©IS831/Image Source; p. 111 (BL): Alamy/©pumkinpie; p. 111 (BR): Alamy/©Anatolii Babii; p. 112 (TL): Shutterstock Images/Jag_cz; p. 112 (TR): Shutterstock Images/Matteo photos; p. 112 (BL): Shutterstock Images/Lisa F. Young; p. 112 (BR): Alamy/©Sigrid Olsson/PhotoAlto; p. 113 (TL): Alamy/©David L. Moore - Lifestyle; p. 113 (BL): Shutterstock Images/OLJ Studio; p. 113 (TR): Corbis/David Lefranc; p. 113 (BR): Shutterstock Images/BKMCphotography; p. 114 (TR): Alamy/©John Elk III; p. 114 (TL): Shutterstock Images/Dja65; p. 115 (T): Getty Images/peplow/iStock/360; p. 117 (TR): Bridgeman Art Library / Musee Marmottan, Paris, France / Giraudon; p. 117(BL): Alamy/©Painting; p. 119 (TL): Alamy/©emanja Radovanovic; p. 120 (L1): Getty Images/Songquan Deng/iStock/360; p. 120 (L2): Getty Images/Matthew Dixon/iStock/360; p. 120 (R1): Alamy/©Geoff Marshall; p. 120 (R2): Shutterstock Images/Art Konovalov; p. 121 (TR): Getty Images/Christopher Futcher/iStock/360; p. 121 (CR): Shutterstock Images/febri ardi Antonius; p. 122 (C):Alamy/©Paul Lindsay; p. 122 (TC): Shutterstock Images/jaroslava V; p. 123 (TL): actionplus sports images; p. 123 (CL): Alamy/©Stephen Barnes/Sport; p. 124 (C): Getty Images/Matthew Stockman/Getty Images Sport; p. 125 (TL): Corbis/Lea Suzuki/San Francisco Chronicle; p. 125 (TR): Superstock/Science and Society/Science and Society; p. 125 (BR): Shutterstock Images/Serdiukov; p. 125 (CR): Shutterstock Images/ Matusciac Alexandru; p. 125 (CL): Shutterstock Images/Viktor Prymachenko; p. 125 (BL): Shutterstock Images/Africa Studio.

The publishers are grateful to the following illustrators:
David Belmonte (Beehive Illustration): p. 116; Anni Betts p. 4, 38; Nigel Dobbyn (Beehive Illustration): p. 78; Mark Duffin p. 12, 116; Guy Pearce p. 35; Sean Tiffany p. 5; Q2A Media Services, Inc. p. 5, 14, 15, 24, 36, 37, 46, 47, 58, 68, 80, 90, 91, 118; Tony Wilkins p. 115, 118.

All video stills by kind permission of:
Discovery Communications, LLC 2015: p. 8(1, 2, 4), 11, 14, 18 (1, 2, 4), 21, 24, 30 (1, 2, 4), 33, 36, 40 (1, 2, 4), 43, 46, 52 (1, 2, 4), 55, 58, 62 (1, 2, 4), 65, 68, 74 (1, 2, 4), 77, 80, 84 (1, 2, 4), 87, 90, 115, 116, 117, 118, 119, 120, 121, 122.
Cambridge University Press: 7, 8 (3), 16, 18 (3), 26, 30 (3), 38, 40 (3), 48, 52 (3), 60, 62 (3), 70, 74 (3), 84 (3), 92.

Corpus
Development of this publication has made use of the Cambridge English Corpus (CEC). The CEC is a computer database of contemporary spoken and written English, which currently stands at over one billion words. It includes British English, American English and other varieties of English. It also includes the Cambridge Learner Corpus, developed in collaboration with the University of Cambridge ESOL Examinations. Cambridge University Press has built up the CEC to provide evidence about language use that helps to produce better language teaching materials.

The publishers are grateful to the following contributors:
Blooberry: concept design
emc design limited: text design and layouts
QBS Learning: cover design and photo selection
Ian Harker and Dave Morritt at DSound: audio recordings
Integra: video production
Nick Bruckman and People's TV: voxpop video production
Hart McCleod: video voiceovers
Anna Whitcher: video management
BraveArts, S.L: additional audio recordings
Getty Images: music
Vicki Anderson: Speaking and Writing pages
Debbie Owen and Alice Martin: Starter Unit
Jose Luis Jiménez Maroto and Alice Martin: CLIL pages
Mick Green: Grammar Reference pages
Emma Szlachta: Editor & Vocabulary Bank
Debbie Owen and Alice Martin: Project pages
Diane Nicholls: Corpus research & Get it Right features

This page is intentionally left blank

Eyes Open 3 Combo B
WORKBOOK

Vicki Anderson with Eoin Higgins

CAMBRIDGE UNIVERSITY PRESS

Discovery EDUCATION

Contents

5 Let's talk — page 47

6 Fears — page 57

7 School life — page 67

8 Green planet — page 77

Speaking extra — page 92

Language focus extra — page 100

5 Let's talk

Vocabulary

Communication

1 ★ **Match the words and phrases with the correct definitions.**

1. the name of a post on Twitter — _d_
2. something you write, send and receive on your mobile phone ___
3. something you write, send and receive on your computer or on the Internet ___
4. to speak informally to someone face-to-face ___
5. a place for online discussion with lots of people ___
6. to speak to (and see) someone computer to computer ___
7. a personal website that gives regular information to readers ___
8. a website that allows users to communicate with each other by posting information, photos and messages ___
9. a short message on a social network site ___

a email   f post
b chat   g forum
c text message   h Skype™
d Tweet   i social network
e blog

2 ★ **Write communication words from Exercise 1 next to the correct definitions.**

1. the name of a post on Twitter — _Tweet_
2. something you write, send and receive on your mobile phone ___
3. speaking informally to someone face to face ___
4. a place for online discussion with lots of people ___
5. speak to (and see) someone computer to computer ___
6. a website that gives readers regular information ___

3 ★★ **Complete the text about how Josh's brother communicates.**

My brother is a university student but he doesn't study much. When he gets up he goes on Twitter to read all the ¹ _Tweets_ from people he follows. After breakfast he writes a(n) ² _____ – he usually talks about university life. He reads all the ³ _____ he's got on Facebook. Then he reads and answers any ⁴ _____ too, but he says a lot of them are junk with adverts for things he's not interested in. He also spends time on a skateboard ⁵ _____ talking to skaters from all over the world. In the evening we often talk on ⁶ _____ (he helps me with my homework!). When he goes out with his friends, they use WhatsApp and organise it by ⁷ _____ . So my brother does a lot of communicating. The funny thing is, he's got a mobile phone and a home phone, but he never makes any ⁸ _____ !

4 ★★★ **How do you and your friends communicate? Answer the questions and write at least five sentences.**

1. Which ways to communicate are the most popular with you and your friends? Why?
2. Did you use the same ones last year? Why?/Why not?
3. Are there any you never use? Why not?
4. How do your parents and grandparents communicate? Is it the same as you?

I usually use text messages on my mobile to talk to my friends because ...

Language focus 1

will, might, may + adverbs of possibility

1 ★ Circle the correct words in the table.

1	Use *will* to show we are **sure** / **not sure** about the future.
2	Use *might* to show we are **sure** / **not sure** about the future.
3	The negative of *will* is **don't will** / **won't**.
4	The negative of *might* is **don't might** / **might not**.
5	Use *will* or *might* + **infinitive** / **-ing** form.

2 ★★ Complete the sentences with the correct form of *will* or *might*.

1 I'm not sure, but my parents ___might___ give me a smartphone for my birthday.
2 He's not answering his email. He _____ be on holiday. I don't know.
3 There _____ be enough time to discuss it in class, so let's talk about it on the forum.
4 She _____ be able to phone you. I don't know if her mobile works there.
5 I'm sure Amy _____ post the photos on Facebook so that we can all see them.

3 ★★ Read the rules. Are they true (*T*) or false (*F*)?

1 We use *definitely* and *certainly* when we are very sure of the future. ___T___
2 When we are less sure of the future, we use *probably*. ___
3 We can't use these adverbs with negative verbs. ___
4 We can use these adverbs with *might (not)*. ___
5 With affirmative verbs the adverb goes before *will*. ___
6 With negative verbs the adverb goes before *won't*. ___

4 ★★★ Complete the email about Gina's plans. Use the verbs in the box with *might* or *will*, and the adverbs in brackets.

> ~~visit~~   not come   not have to   not be
> agree   stay   have   be

Hi Jo,
How are things? I've got some great news! Keira and I ¹ _will definitely visit_ (definitely) our grandparents in July. We ² _____ (certainly) for three weeks, and maybe longer if we can. ³ _____ you _____ there in July? I hope so! My dad ⁴ _____ (definitely) with us because he's working, but Mum ⁵ _____ work all of July and so maybe she can join us later.

The other news is that I ⁶ _____ a party for my birthday. Dad has said yes but Mum hasn't decided yet. It's OK, I think she ⁷ _____ (probably) soon! If I do have one, can you come? You can stay the weekend. Please say yes! It ⁸ _____ (certainly) the same without you!

Gina

5 ★★★ Write at least five sentences about you and your life. Use *will*, *might* and adverbs of probability and possibility. Use the ideas in the box or your own ideas.

> play a (sport) match   go to the cinema   go swimming
> spend a day at the beach   visit my grandparents
> buy a new game

I might go swimming with my friends on Saturday.

Explore communications collocations

6 ★★ Circle the correct options.

1 A lot of my **virtual** / **computer** friends are also friends in real life.
2 I try not to look at **social** / **friend** network sites when I'm doing my homework.
3 My last status **update** / **post** just said 'Help!' – I was doing my homework!
4 My dad says we are the **digital** / **network** generation because we don't know a world without computers.
5 Sometimes it's better to talk **face-** / **head-** to-face than online.

48   Unit 5

Listening and vocabulary

Listening

1 ★ 🔊 05 **Listen to Olga and Tanya discussing something Tanya has done. Which sentence is true?**
a Tanya has stopped using Facebook for a month.
b Tanya has decided never to use Facebook again.
c Tanya has received a lot of insulting Tweets.

2 ★★ 🔊 05 **Read the sentences. Listen again and circle the correct options.**
1 Olga tried to go on Tanya's Facebook page to **say happy birthday** / post a website link.
2 Tanya thinks she **should / shouldn't** spend less time on Facebook.
3 Tanya wants to spend more time socialising with her **school friends / real friends**.
4 Tanya thinks that some of the posts she reads are **private / not true**.
5 A friend of Olga's **sent insults / received insults** on Twitter.
6 Olga doesn't think Tanya needs to **stop using Facebook / use Facebook any more**.
7 Tanya is worried about people seeing **her private details / her friends' Facebook pages**.
8 Tanya plans to spend more time **chatting to her friends / using different social networks**.
9 Tanya is **sure / not sure** what she's going to do at the end of her experiment.
10 Olga is going to contact Tanya on **Facebook / Skype™** later.

Communication verbs

3 ★ **Write the verbs in the box next to the correct definitions.**

> whisper   complain   boast   gossip
> argue   joke   shout   criticise

1 disagree with someone, sometimes loudly or aggressively — _argue_
2 say how good you are at doing something _____
3 say something funny _____
4 talk very quietly so other people can't hear _____
5 talk very loudly _____
6 talk about other people _____
7 say negative things about someone _____
8 say that you don't like something _____

4 ★★ **Complete the text with the correct form of the verbs in Exercise 3.**

I've got a great group of friends I've known since primary school. We always meet at the weekend to laugh and ¹ _joke_ , and ² _____ about people we know. My friends never ³ _____ me for what I wear or ⁴ _____ about me in front of me. They like me for who I am. We know each other well, too. Alicia ⁵ _____ that she's the best basketball player in the school, and Nuria and I ⁶ _____ that our parents are too strict. Sometimes we ⁷ _____ about where to meet and what to do, but we never get angry or ⁸ _____ and we always agree in the end.

Language focus 2

First conditional + *may/might, be able to*

1 ★ Match the sentence halves.
1 If you phone me tonight, _b_
2 If we start a class blog, __
3 She may not stay on Twitter __
4 If you post the photos on Facebook, __
5 Will you send me the stuff by email __
6 I won't know their address __

a if you have time?
b I might not have time to talk to you.
c everyone will be able to see them.
d will everyone post on it?
e if they don't text me.
f if people insult her.

2 ★★ Put the verbs in brackets in the correct form to complete this chain of events. Use the verb prompts in brackets to help you.

Now the problem is … If I ¹____put____ (put) my party on Facebook, all my friends ² _____ (see) it – and I've got 217! If everyone ³ _____ (see) it, they ⁴ _____ (might/think) it's an open invitation. If they ⁵ _____ (think) it's an open invitation, they ⁶ _____ (may/invite) more people. And if they ⁷ _____ (invite) more people, everyone ⁸ _____ (might/decide) to come and I ⁹ _____ (not/have) enough room for them. If too many people ¹⁰ _____ (come), they ¹¹ _____ (may/break) things. And if they ¹² _____ (break) things and my parents ¹³ _____ (find out), I ¹⁴ _____ (not/be able to) have any more parties!

3 ★★ Complete the conversation with the correct form of the verbs in the box. Use *may* or *might* when the person is not sure.

~~know~~ talk whisper think be
~~ask~~ give tell hear not buy

Tim: What shall we get Dad for his birthday? He's 40!
Sara: No idea. Let's ask him.
Tim: No, if we ¹ _ask_ him, he ² _will know_ what his present is. That's boring. If we ³ _____ him a surprise, I don't know – it ⁴ _____ more fun!
Sara: Yes, but if he ⁵ _____ us, we ⁶ _____ him something he doesn't like.
Tim: Well, we could ask Mum, she'll know!
Sara: OK, good idea! If you ⁷ _____ to her now, I don't think Dad ⁸ _____ you. But whisper!
Tim: Don't be silly! If I ⁹ _____ , he ¹⁰ _____ something mysterious is going on, don't you think?

4 ★★★ Write a chain of events like the one in Exercise 3. Use one of the ideas below or your own idea. How long can you make the chain?

If I finish my homework quickly, …
If my parents allow me to …
If I lose my mobile phone, …

Explore phrasal verbs (2)

5 ★★ Match the sentence halves.
1 Do you think this app will _e_
2 English is very flexible so we keep on adding __
3 Does anyone know when social networks __
4 The number of people on social network sites __
5 I speak German so when we went to Berlin __

a is going up every year.
b I was able to get by.
c new words to the language.
d started coming into use?
e turn into the next popular thing?

50 Unit 5

Reading

1 ★ Read the text about Tony Anderson. How has the Internet changed his life?

BREAKING DOWN THE BARRIERS!

Tony Anderson is 15 and, like most people his age, he spends a lot of time on his computer and smartphone, but his parents aren't complaining. In fact, they're pleased. This is because Tony was born **deaf**, but now, thanks to technology and social media, his life has completely changed. Young deaf people have attended the same schools as other children for a long time, but in the past they found it difficult to make friends. Most deaf people could only communicate using sign language, and so their classmates couldn't talk to them. And if you can't communicate, you won't be able to **take part** in social activities with other teenagers. So deaf teenagers felt **isolated** and bored, didn't have a social life, and often suffered from low self-esteem.

Then along came the technological revolution, with computers, the Internet and mobile phones. Teenagers began to communicate more and more by text message and go on social media sites like Facebook and Twitter. For deaf teenagers, the Internet is an ideal way to communicate, because it doesn't need hearing or speaking. More importantly, everyone uses it, not just deaf people. As Tony explains, 'Now, if you're a deaf teenager, no-one will know you're different. It's incredible! I can post on chat forums or social networks and the other people probably won't know I'm deaf, so they **treat** me like everyone else. It's made me a lot more relaxed and confident.'

The other thing Tony enjoys is being able to connect up with other teenagers who are deaf. 'We've all had similar experiences in life, so we understand each other. I've made some good friends online, and sometimes we **meet up**, too. One day soon, deaf teenagers might be able to have a totally normal social life because of the Internet!'

2 ★★ Complete the sentences with the words in *bold* from the text.

1 Let's _____ tomorrow morning and go to the comic exhibition.
2 Would you like to _____ in an experiment?
3 Mark was ill when he was a baby and now he is _____ in one ear.
4 You mustn't _____ your brother like that! Be nice to him.
5 We lived in a remote place and I felt very _____ .

3 ★★ Read the text again and circle the correct options.

1 Why does Tony spend a lot of time on his computer?
  a He's a typical teenager.
  b He doesn't do any school work.
  c He hasn't got a mobile phone.
2 Why were deaf teenagers often unhappy before the Internet?
  a Schools didn't know how to teach them.
  b They didn't have any friends.
  c It was difficult to communicate with others.
3 What was not true for deaf teenagers before technology?
  a They didn't often go out with friends.
  b A lot of them didn't have much confidence.
  c They all had to communicate with sign language.
4 Why is technology so important for Tony?
  a It means he's like other teenagers.
  b He's good at it because he's deaf.
  c He can explain to people that he's deaf.
5 What is not true about Tony's life nowadays?
  a He's got a normal social life.
  b He doesn't know any other deaf teenagers.
  c He feels better about himself.

4 ★★★ Read the summary of the text. Correct five mistakes.

Tony Anderson is a deaf teenager who uses the Internet and social networks to make friends and ¹to go to school. His parents ²are worried about him spending a lot of time on the Internet because it has helped Tony in his social life and ³in sports. Now with the Internet and mobile phones people ⁴still know he's deaf and he can communicate with other people. He's made a lot of friends and some of his new friends are deaf. ⁵He'd like to meet up with them.

1 _____have a social life_____
2 _____
3 _____
4 _____
5 _____

5 ★★★ Tony's story shows a positive aspect of the Internet. What other good things are there? Write at least three more advantages.

The Internet helps young people in different cities or countries communicate.

Unit 5 51

Writing

An essay

1 Read Harry's essay. Does he agree or disagree with the essay title?

TEENAGERS USE SOCIAL MEDIA SITES TOO MUCH. DISCUSS.

A Thousands of teenagers post on social networks every day. In fact, it has become the most popular way for them to communicate. Why is it so popular, and do we use it too much?

B ¹ _Firstly_ , social networks are a quick, easy and cheap way to tell your friends your news. You can ² _____ post photos and weblinks, and share music and video clips. ³ _____ , you can combine it with other computer activities.

C ⁴ _____ there are negatives, too. ⁵ _____ , a lot of 'friends' aren't friends at all. If you aren't careful, you'll share personal information with complete strangers. ⁶ _____ , some people might only socialise online.

D On balance, I don't think teenagers use these sites too much, and we still meet our friends face to face.

2 Complete Harry's essay about social media. Use the words in the box.

> ~~firstly~~   lastly   also   for one thing   in addition   on the other hand

3 Read the essay again. Complete the notes in the table.

Facts to introduce the topic	Positive arguments
1 _thousands of teenagers_ post on social networks every day 2 has become the most popular way _____	3 quick, easy and _____ 4 _____ photos and links, _____ music and video clips 5 _____ it with other computer activities
Negative arguments	**Harry's opinion and why**
6 some _____ aren't friends at all 7 you should be _____ with personal information 8 some people might only _____	9 teens _____ these sites too much 10 still meet _____

Useful language — Introducing points and arguments

4 Complete the table with the words in the box and the words in Exercise 2.

> ~~however~~   nevertheless   what's more   on one hand

Ordering points	Adding points	Introducing arguments	Contrasting arguments
_____	_____	_____	_however_
_____	_____	_____	_____
	_____		_____

52 Unit 5

Writing

5 Put the words in order to make essay introduction questions.
1. places / Are / social / dangerous / networks / ?
   Are social networks dangerous places?
2. age / you / Should / everyone / your / tell / ?
   _____
3. safe / information / share / Is / to / it / personal / ?
   _____
4. it / a / photos / social / idea / to / network / post / Is / good / on / a / ?
   _____

> **WRITING TIP**
> Make it better! ✓ ✓ ✓
> It's always better to make sure general statements don't mean *everyone*, *everything* or *always*.

6 Put the words in brackets in the correct place in the general statements.
1. Teenagers should ˄avoid putting photos of themselves on the Internet. (generally) [*generally* inserted before *avoid*]
2. People share all sorts of information on social networks. (may)
3. We shouldn't post any information about ourselves online. (perhaps)
4. Other people find out all about you from your Facebook profile. (can)

> **WRITING TIP**
> Make it better! ✓ ✓ ✓
> Give your own opinion and use different expressions.

7 Read the sentences. Which one does **not** give an opinion?
1. I don't really think people know about the dangers of Facebook.
2. In my view, it is very dangerous to put personal information on social network sites.
3. There have been many stories of people using other people's personal information online.
4. In my opinion, social networking sites are not safe.
5. I believe it's good to learn how to use these sites.

8 When you write an essay you should include four paragraphs. Complete the sentences with the words in the box.

| against | conclusion | ~~introduction~~ |
| opinion | favour | |

1. Paragraph A is the ___introduction___ .
2. Paragraph B gives arguments in _____ .
3. Paragraph C gives arguments _____ .
4. Paragraph D gives the _____ , including your _____ .

PLAN

9 You are going to write an essay with the title: 'It is dangerous to put too much personal information on social networking sites. Discuss.' Use the paragraphs in Exercise 8 and your own ideas to make notes.

WRITE

10 Write your essay. Look at page 61 of the Student's Book to help you.

_____
_____
_____
_____
_____
_____
_____
_____
_____
_____
_____
_____
_____
_____
_____
_____
_____

CHECK

11 Check your writing. Can you say YES to these questions?
- Have you included all the paragraphs in Exercise 8?
- Have you introduced your points and arguments?
- Have you used a question in the introduction?
- Have you made sure general statements don't mean *everyone*, *everything* or *always*?
- Have you given your own opinion?
- Are the spelling and punctuation correct?

Do you need to write a second draft?

5 Review

Vocabulary
Communication

1 Are these sentences true (*T*) or false (*F*)?
1 You can send photos and documents by email. _T_
2 You can join a discussion group on a forum. ___
3 You can send Tweets to a large group of people on Twitter. ___
4 You can speak and listen to someone with text messages. ___
5 You can write a blog post to tell other people about your life. ___
6 You can have a live chat with someone on a forum. ___

Total: 5

Communication verbs

2 Complete the sentences with the words in the box.

| boast   argue   ~~whisper~~   complain   joke   shout |

1 Don't talk so loudly – you should always _whisper_ in the library.
2 I don't want to _____ , but I'm very good at repairing computers.
3 We shouldn't _____ about the food. At least it's not very expensive.
4 They tried to _____ about it, but he was really upset and didn't laugh.
5 There's no need to _____ – I can hear you very well!
6 I know we disagree sometimes, but I don't want to _____ .

Total: 5

Language focus
will, *may*, *might* + adverbs of possibility

3 Match the sentence halves.
1 Everyone will definitely _d_
2 Our parents might not ___
3 How might the world be different ___
4 I'll probably Skype™ you later ___
5 Social networks certainly won't replace ___
6 Will you write ___

a to talk about the party.
b face-to-face communications.
c ever understand Facebook.
d use social media in the future.
e blog posts on holiday?
f in 50 years' time?

Total: 5

First conditional + *may/might*, *be able to*

4 Complete the first conditional sentences with the correct form of the verbs in brackets. Use *may* or *might* when the person is not sure.
1 If you ___*give*___ (give) me your email address, I'll ___*send*___ (send) you an email about the party.
2 I think she _____ (be) very upset if I _____ (not reply) to her email.
3 If I _____ (invite) everyone on Facebook, there _____ (be) too many people.
4 _____ (you send) me a text message if you _____ (get) home late?
5 It's possible he _____ (get) a better job if he _____ (learn) more about computers.
6 If you _____ (work) harder at home, you _____ (not have) the same problems in class. I'm not sure though.

Total: 5

Language builder

5 Complete the conversation with the missing words. Circle the correct options.

Dave: What ¹___ just now?
Tom: I ²___ my text messages.
Dave: How often ³___ check your messages?
Tom: Once or twice an hour. My mum ⁴___ me a message about helping her to wash the car this afternoon.
Dave: I hate having to help around the house! Do you think robots ⁵___ do all our work for us in the future?
Tom: I'm not sure. I think we ⁶___ robots in hospitals and maybe in schools.
Dave: If we ⁷___ robots in schools, we ⁸___ need teachers any more.
Tom: I'm not sure about that. We ⁹___ teachers, but we ¹⁰___ talk to them on Skype™.

1	a	you were doing	**b**	**were you doing**	c you doing
2	a	was checking	b	'm checking	c check
3	a	do usually you	b	usually do you	c do you usually
4	a	just has sent	b	has just sent	c has sent just
5	a	will	b	won't	c are
6	a	'll certainly have	b	certainly will have	c 'll have certainly
7	a	have	b	'll have	c 'd have
8	a	will	b	might not	c don't
9	a	'll definitely need	b	might need definitely	c definitely might need
10	a	might have	b	might have to	c have to

Total: 9

Vocabulary builder

6 Circle the correct options.

1 Sometimes it's better to talk face-___-face.
　a on　　b by　　**c to**
2 Abby sent a very funny text ___ last night. Look.
　a network　b post　c message
3 Eva posted a photo of the ___ park on Facebook.
　a theme　b summer　c guided
4 Don't worry, it's not true. I'm only ___ !
　a gossiping　b joking　c whispering
5 Could you please ___ your bedroom? It's a mess.
　a pick up　b set up　c tidy up
6 I'm going ___ for clothes tomorrow.
　a shopping　b getting　c buying
7 Have you seen the new ___ on our school wall?
　a sculpture　b paint　c mural
8 Stop ___ . I can hear you in my bedroom!
　a boasting　b arguing　c shouting
9 The number of students in our school has ___ in the last few years.
　a gone up　b kept on　c shown up
10 I'd like to relax and ___ at the beach for a few hours.
　a pick up　b get by　c chill out

Total: 9

Speaking

7 Put the sentences in the correct order to make a conversation.

___ Lynn: Listen, I think I can help you. Let's practise some test questions together.
___ Lynn: Don't worry! Of course you will!
_1_ Lynn: What's the matter Sally? You look worried.
___ Lynn: No, you're not. It'll turn out all right.
___ Sally: I've got a test tomorrow and I'm really worried I won't pass.
___ Sally: I don't think it will. It never does.
___ Sally: OK! That sounds like a good idea.
___ Sally: You know I'm really bad at Maths.

Total: 7

Total: 45

Unit 5 Review　55

Get it right! Unit 5

will, might/may + adverbs of possibility

1 Circle the correct options.
During my trip to London …
1 I might **going** / **go** / **went** to an art gallery.
2 I will **visited** / **visiting** / **visit** my uncle.
3 I might **sent** / **send** / **sending** some postcards.
4 I will **buying** / **buy** / **bought** some souvenirs.
5 I might **take** / **taking** / **took** a boat trip.
6 I will **phoning** / **phone** / **phoned** my parents every day.

First conditional

> Remember that:
> - we use *if* + subject + the present simple in the action/situation clause
>   ✓ *If I'm late, I will send you a text.*
> - we use *will/won't* + infinitive to talk about the consequences of the action/situation
>   ✓ *If I'm late, I will send you a text.*
>   ✗ *If I am late, I send you a text.*
> - We don't use *will/won't* in the same clause as *if*.
>   ✓ *If I'm late, I will send you a text.*
>   ✗ *If I will be late, I will send you a text.*

2 Complete the sentences with the correct form of the verb in brackets and *will* if needed.
1 If I ___find___ (find) the information, I ___will call___ (call) you.
2 If I _____ (have) time, I _____ (come) to see you on Saturday.
3 I _____ (meet) you after school if you _____ (want) me to.
4 If Lara _____ (be) ill, we _____ (not go) to the cinema tonight.
5 You _____ (not pass) your exams if you _____ (not work) hard.

at the moment/in the future

> Remember that:
> - we use *in the future* to talk about what will happen in a period of time that is to come
>   ✓ *Tablets will be popular in the future.*
>   ✗ *Tablets will be popular at the future.*
> - we use *at the moment* to talk about what is happening now
>   ✓ *Smartphones are popular at the moment.*
>   ✗ *Smartphones are popular at moment.*

3 Find and correct four more mistakes with *at the moment/in the future* in the text.

> Marcus: Hi Helen, what are you studying **at** ~~in~~ the moment?
> Helen: I'm reading about social networks for a school project.
> Marcus: That's interesting. Do you use any social networks?
> Helen: Well, at moment, I only use them to keep in contact with my cousins. But a lot of my friends use Facebook now, so I might use it more on the future. What about you?
> Marcus: Oh, I'm not on any social networks on the moment, but I think the future it will be important for my job.

complain

> Remember that:
> - the infinitive of the verb is *complain*; the *-ing* form is *complaining*, and the past simple is *complained*
>   ✓ *He complained about the noise in the classroom.*
>   ✗ *He complaint about the noise in the classroom.*
> - we use *about* after *complain* to talk about things we do not like
>   ✓ *He complained about the noise in the classroom.*
>   ✗ *He complained for the noise in the classroom.*
>   ✗ *He complained with the noise in the classroom.*

4 Are the sentences correct? Correct the incorrect sentences.
1 When was the last time you complaint for something?
   When was the last time you complained about something?
2 Jane is always complaining about her sister.
   _____
3 You shouldn't have complainted! Now they'll be angry.
   _____
4 My parents complain about the time I spend on Facebook.
   _____
5 I don't know what you're complaining with. It's great here!
   _____
6 They complaint for the homework, but the teacher didn't listen.
   _____

56 Get it right! 5

6 Fears

Vocabulary

Fears

1 ★ Put the letters in order to make eight fears. Then write them under the correct pictures.

> bdirs   flist   het adkr   ceinsst
> fgilny   aeknss   eghhist   cwnsol

1 _flying_
2 _____ 
3 _____ 
4 _____ 
5 _____ 
6 _____ 
7 _____ 
8 _____ 

2 ★★ Complete the sentences with the fears from Exercise 1.
1 Tobey Maguire, the Spider-Man actor, is afraid of _heights_ and tall buildings!
2 The Malayan Blue Krait is one of the most venomous _____ in the world.
3 City people often complain that the _____ sing too loudly in the country.
4 To get to the top of the Empire State Building you have to take two _____ . They aren't quick – the total time is 1½ minutes.
5 Mosquitoes are the most dangerous _____ in the world as they carry malaria.
6 According to statistics, _____ is safer than driving or going by coach.
7 The organisation '_____ without Borders' makes people in difficult situations laugh.
8 At night, when you are in _____ , noises sound a lot louder than during the day.

3 ★★ Complete the text about an awful holiday.
What a holiday! My dad is terrified of ¹_flying_ so we went to Spain on a coach – 33 hours! The hotel was great, but we were on the fourteenth floor. My mum refused to go in the ²_____ as she's claustrophobic. Luckily the hotel moved us to the second floor and she used the stairs. I had to share a room with my brother. He's scared of ³_____ so he slept with the lights on, but I couldn't go to sleep. Then the ⁴_____ outside woke me up at five every morning! One day, on a guided tour, we had to walk up a mountain path. My dad really doesn't like ⁵_____ and didn't go up, and my mum decided she heard ⁶_____ moving in the grass and went back down. We had a picnic lunch but there were tiny flying ⁷_____ everywhere. It was horrible! At least the ⁸_____ at the circus made everyone laugh. No-one in my family is afraid of them!

4 ★★★ Can you imagine why people are afraid of these things? Write at least five sentences. Use the ideas in the box or your own ideas.

> they bite   they move fast   you could fall
> you could crash   dangerous   they attack
> imagine monsters   wear a strange costume

People are afraid of insects because they bite and have got a lot of legs.

Unit 6   57

Language focus 1

be going to / will / Present continuous

1 ★ Circle the correct words.
1. Use **will** / **going to** / **the present continuous** for personal intentions.
2. Use **will** / **going to** / **the present continuous** for predictions.
3. Use **will** / **going to** / **the present continuous** for definite arrangements.

2 ★★ Write sentences about the future. Use *will*, *going to* or the present continuous.
1. I / visit / my cousin / in July (definite arrangement)
   I'm going to visit my cousin in July.
2. This social network / be / very popular / with teenagers (prediction)
   _____
3. Hugh / sing / a song / at the school concert (definite arrangement)
   _____
4. My dad / definitely / not / pick up the spider (prediction)
   _____
5. I / complain / to the director about the lifts (intention)
   _____
6. Harry / post / a Tweet / about the judo competition (intention)
   _____

3 ★★ Complete the conversation with a future form of the verbs in the box or a short answer.

> be   can   ~~spend~~   go (x2)   not go
> write   leave   take

A: Where ¹ *are you going to spend* Easter?
B: Karin and I ² _____ on an adventure holiday.
A: Fantastic! What activities are there?
B: Oh, lots! Look, here's the information. But I ³ _____ rock climbing. I hate heights.
A: Oh, wow! There's sailing! ⁴ _____ sailing?
B: No, I ⁵ _____ . I can't swim and we ⁶ _____ too busy with the other activities!
A: So when ⁷ _____ ?
B: We ⁸ _____ the bus on Friday evening.
A: Well, send us some photos.
B: I don't think we ⁹ _____ post photos – there's no Internet! But I ¹⁰ _____ a blog post about it when I get back.

4 ★★ Complete the text with the correct future form of the verbs in brackets.
I've just finished talking to the doctor about my snake phobia. He says he ¹ *'ll be able to* (can) help me. Did I tell you that I ² _____ (go) on holiday to the Amazon in the summer? I really need help! There ³ _____ (be) snakes everywhere, I'm sure!
The treatment ⁴ _____ (start) on Friday and it ⁵ _____ (be) really difficult. In the first session we ⁶ _____ (go) to the zoo to look at snakes. Ugh! Then the week after the doctor ⁷ _____ (take) a snake out of its tank and we ⁹ _____ (take) it in turns to hold it. I think I ¹⁰ _____ (wear) gloves that day!

5 ★★★ Answer the questions with *will*, *going to* or the present continuous.
1. What arrangements have you got this week?
2. What aren't you planning to do in the near future?
3. What do you think the weather will be like next weekend?

Explore prepositional phrases

6 ★★ Circle the correct options.
1. My mum's terrified **in** / **of** birds so we can't have one as a pet.
2. Dean says he's very embarrassed **of** / **about** the photos on his Facebook post.
3. I can't think **in** / **of** anything to write about for my blog.
4. Clara say she's got a phobia but she doesn't want to share it **about** / **with** us.
5. Don't worry **about** / **with** taking the lift. It'll be fine.

Listening and vocabulary

Listening

1 ★ 🔊 06 **Listen to Jordan talking about a course he's attending. What is the course about? Does he feel positive or negative about it?**

2 ★★ 🔊 06 **Listen again. Are these sentences true (T) or false (F)?**

1 Jordan's phobia started after a visit to the country. _F_
2 He finally decided to do something after a terrifying weekend. ___
3 The course was at a hospital. ___
4 The other people on the course were relaxed. ___
5 The course helps people lose their spider phobia in three sessions. ___
6 A therapist talked about why people get phobias. ___
7 The expert explained two facts about spiders. ___
8 There are many dangerous spiders in Britain. ___
9 Jordan is the only person who is going to have hypnotherapy. ___
10 Jordan is thinking about bringing a pet spider home. ___

-ed and -ing adjective endings

3 ★ **Match the pairs of adjectives with the pictures.**

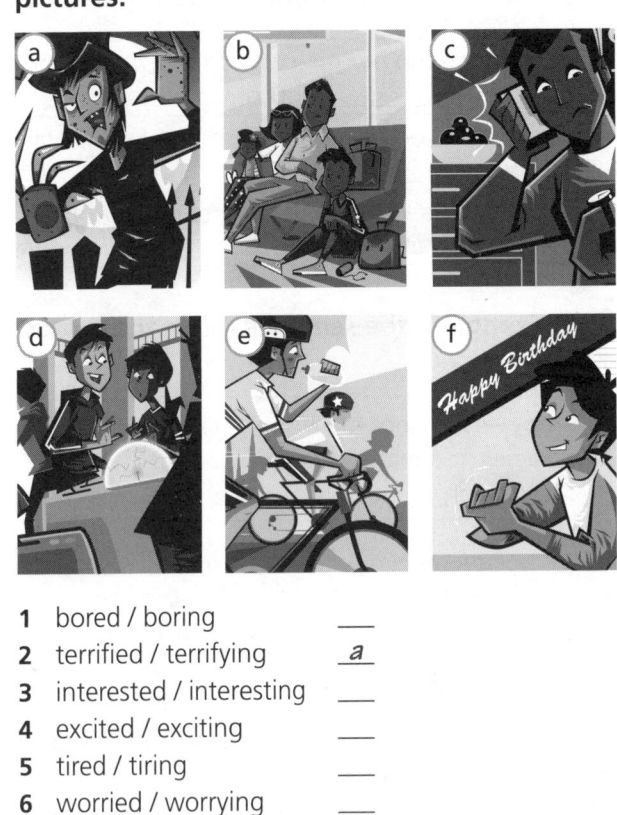

1 bored / boring ___
2 terrified / terrifying _a_
3 interested / interesting ___
4 excited / exciting ___
5 tired / tiring ___
6 worried / worrying ___

4 ★★ **For each pair of gaps, write the -ed or -ing adjective.**

1 a Do we have to go to the concert? Their music is really __boring__ .
  b We've been on this train for five hours. I'm totally __bored__ .
2 a Aaagh! Look at that enormous spider! I'm _____ of spiders.
  b The rollercoaster was _____ . I'm never going on it again.
3 a You went to bed very late last night. Aren't you _____ ?
  b We've got a new athletics coach. Her training sessions are really _____ .
4 a I've never been to a big football match before. I'm so _____ !
  b The kayaking trip was very _____ .
5 a I think climate change is _____ .
  b What a difficult exam. I'm _____ that I've failed it.
6 a This article about phobias is very _____ .
  b I've got a DVD about insects out of the library. Are you _____ ?

Unit 6 59

Language focus 2

Quantifiers

1 ★ Complete the rules in the table. Write *all*, *plural*, *countable* or *uncountable*.

1	We use *too much*, *not much* and *how much* with _____ nouns.
2	We use *too many*, *not many* and *how many* with _____ nouns.
3	We use *a lot of*, *some*, *any*, *enough*, *not enough* and *not any* with _____ nouns.

2 ★ Complete the sentences with the words in the box.

> ~~how many~~   not many   any (x2)
> some   too many   enough
> too much   much   how much

1. ___How many___ dangerous snakes are there in the world?
2. I've studied for 10 hours this week but I still haven't done _____ work. I'm going to fail!
3. Are there _____ clowns at this circus? Yes? Then I don't want to go.
4. _____ money have you got? I need to buy this book for school.
5. A lot of people are afraid of spiders but _____ people have got a phobia of mirrors. It's very unusual.
6. Maybe teenagers spend _____ time on their games consoles.
7. _____ people get very anxious if they can't use their mobile. It's called nomophobia!
8. Holly isn't going to come for a walk. She says there are _____ snakes round here.
9. There aren't _____ insects outside now. In the winter they all die.
10. I haven't got _____ time, but I've got enough to watch the end of this programme.

a little / a few

3 ★ Circle the correct words in the table.

1	Use *a few* and *a little* to talk about **small / large** quantities and amounts.
2	Use *a few / a little* with plural countable nouns.
3	Use *a few / a little* with uncountable nouns.

4 ★★ Complete the text with *a few* or *a little*.

Why do we love horror films? ¹ ___A few___ people never watch them, but most people like being terrified! We think that ² _____ horror is fun, not scary. A good horror film has got ³ _____ essential ingredients. You need ⁴ _____ horrible surprises, a lot of scary music, ⁵ _____ blood (not too much!), and of course, ⁶ _____ monsters, aliens or zombies. You don't need much money, just mix all these together, and you've got a good film!

5 ★★★ What are the essential ingredients of … ? Choose one of the things in the box. Write four or five ideas, using quantifiers. Include at least one thing you *don't* need.

> a computer game   a comedy programme
> a good book   a perfect birthday party

For a perfect birthday party, you don't need a lot of people, only a few good friends and some great music …

Explore opposites

6 ★★ Complete the sentences with the opposites of the adjectives in the box.

> lucky   ~~bad~~   sensible   unsuccessful
> dangerous   old

1. That film wasn't very ___good___ . Don't go to see it.
2. The lift isn't very _____ . It stops between floors.
3. Greg was very _____ . He won the karate competition!
4. Eddie's house is really cool. It's full of _____ furniture.
5. We went on a skiing holiday but there was no snow! We were very _____ .
6. A lot of people think that being afraid of clowns is very _____ . But it's a real phobia.

Reading

1 ★ Read the text about Janie. What was her problem? Does she still have the problem?

Are you EXAM-PHOBIC?

Janie was a good student. She worked hard in class, and did her homework, but she did badly in exams. Then one day her **mind went blank**. She **froze** and couldn't answer any of the questions.

Most people feel a little nervous before a test. It's normal, and a few nerves can often help you do well. But for some people, like Janie, the anxiety is too strong, and it results in physical symptoms which affect their ability to think. This is called test anxiety.

Test anxiety is when you feel stressed because you have to do well. It can also happen when you sing a solo in a concert, or play an important match. In extreme cases, you **shake**, think you are going to **faint**, or your mind goes blank, like Janie. So what's the solution?

- **STUDY HABITS.** Many students only study for exams the night before. You can reduce test anxiety if you study more regularly. This gives you **confidence**, and means you expect to do well.
- **POSITIVE THINKING.** Negative thoughts, like 'I know I'm going to fail this exam,' affect your confidence in yourself. Repeat positive messages to yourself.
- **LOOK AFTER YOURSELF.** Getting enough sleep and exercise, and eating healthy food before an exam can help your mind work at its best.
- **BREATHE.** Calm yourself with breathing exercises regularly, when you're *not* stressed. Do these exercises before an exam, and your body recognises them as the **signal** to relax.

Janie already had some good study habits, but she didn't get enough sleep. She also expected to do badly in exams. So she used these **tips** to help herself, and they worked! Now she can't believe she ever had test anxiety.

2 ★★ Match the words in the box with the definitions. Use the words in **bold** in the text to help you.

> (mind) go blank   signal   ~~shake~~   faint [verb]
> confidence   tip [noun]   breathe   freeze

1 small uncontrollable movements of the body — _shake_
2 you cannot remember anything — _____
3 a feeling that you can do something well — _____
4 a small piece of advice — _____
5 take air in and out of your body — _____
6 lose consciousness — _____
7 become immobile — _____
8 gesture or action used to give an instruction — _____

3 ★★ Read the text again and answer the questions.
1 Why was it surprising that Janie didn't do well in exams?
   Because she was a good student.
2 Why can a few nerves before an exam be a good thing?
   _____
3 Why can studying more regularly help?
   _____
4 Why should you get enough sleep, food and exercise?
   _____
5 When should you do breathing exercises?
   _____
6 How did Janie solve her problem?
   _____

4 ★★★ Read the sentences. Do these people have test anxiety? Write Yes (Y) or No (N).
1 'I think I'm going to faint!' — Y
2 'I'm going to bed early to get a good night's sleep.' — ___
3 'Oh no! I can't remember anything!' — ___
4 'Before an exam, I do breathing exercises to relax.' — ___
5 'I've worked hard for this exam. I know I can pass.' — ___
6 'I know I'm going to fail. I know it!' — ___

5 ★★★ How do you feel about exams? Have you ever had any of the symptoms in the text? Do you think the solutions would work for you? Why?/Why not? Write your answers.

Writing

An email to a friend

1 Read Eve's email to her friend about her plans. What is she afraid of?

Your MAIL   + New   Reply | ▼   Delete

Hi Lena,

It was great to get your news! ¹**(My news)** / **The fact** is that I'm going to leave the city and move to the country!

My parents have bought a farm (see the photo attached – it's beautiful!) and ²**the truth / the idea** is that we keep cows and horses. It's really exciting, but I'm also worried. ³**My problem / My news** is that I'm terrified of large birds! When I see one I start to shake and feel faint. We went to see the farm yesterday and ⁴**the truth / the idea** was I couldn't relax at all. What can I do?

⁵**The fact / The big news** is that I have to do something or my life will be awful.

Should I tell my parents? What do you think?

Love,

Eve

---

2 Read the email again. Circle the correct options.

3 Read the email again and complete the sentences.
1. Eve ___doesn't live___ in the country now.
2. She and her parents are going to live on a _____ .
3. Eve is _____ about moving.
4. She's afraid of _____ birds.
5. When she sees a bird she thinks she's going to _____ .
6. She saw the farm _____ .
7. On the farm she can't _____ .
8. She _____ told her parents about the problem.

Useful language — Introducing news and explaining things

4 Match the sentences.
1. My big news is that I'm going to spend the summer working at a restaurant.   _b_
2. My news is that my parents are sending me to Ireland for two weeks.   ___
3. The fact is that I'm terrified of the dark.   ___
4. My news is that I'm going to do a course about social networks.   ___
5. The big news is that my family and I are going to live in Canada.   ___

a. The truth is I haven't even got a Facebook account!
b. The problem is that I don't know how to cook!
c. And the truth is that I'm embarrassed about it.
d. The problem is that I hate the winter and the snow!
e. The idea is that I'll live with a family and practise my English.

Writing

5 Choose the correct options.
1. We're going to Los Angeles. I'm really (excited) / exciting.
2. We're moving to another house. It's amazed / amazing.
3. I'm afraid of the dark. I feel really embarrassed / embarrassing.
4. The truth is I hate flying and I'm really worried / worrying.
5. We live on the top floor and it's terrified / terrifying.

6 Are the sentences plans or predictions? Tick (✓) the correct box.

	plan	prediction
1 It'll be really exciting.		✓
2 We're going to live in the country.		
3 My life will be awful!		
4 It'll be a big change for me.		
5 I'm going to have my own room.		
6 My dad's going to work at a different company.		

> **WRITING TIP**
> Make it better! ✓ ✓ ✓
> Ask for advice at the end of your email.

7 Read the sentences. Which sentence does **not** ask for advice?
1. Should I go to a doctor about my problem?
2. I really don't know what to do.
3. What do you think I should do?
4. Do you think I should tell my mother?
5. Is it a good idea to tell someone?

8 Number the things in the list in the order they appear in the email.
what the problem is ___
an introduction _1_
a question to ask what your friend thinks ___
how you feel about the problem and why ___
some personal news ___
what you have/haven't done about the problem ___

PLAN

9 Invent a problem to write about. Make notes for each heading in Exercise 8.

WRITE

10 Write an email to a friend about your problem. Look at page 71 of the Student's Book to help you.

_____
_____
_____
_____
_____
_____
_____
_____
_____
_____
_____
_____
_____
_____
_____
_____
_____

CHECK

11 Check your writing. Can you say YES to these questions?
- Is the information from the list in Exercise 8 in your email?
- Have you used expressions to explain the problem in your email?
- Have you used -ed and -ing adjectives correctly?
- Have you used going to for plans and will for predictions?
- Have you finished your email asking for advice?
- Are the spelling and punctuation correct?

Do you need to write a second draft?

6 Review

Vocabulary
Fears

1 Complete the sentences with the words in the box. There are two extra words.

> snakes flying heights clowns
> insects lifts the dark birds

1 I don't like travelling by plane because I'm afraid of ___flying___ .
2 I hate going to the circus because I'm afraid of _____ .
3 I usually take the stairs to the top floor because I'm afraid of _____ .
4 I don't want to go up the tower because I'm afraid of _____ .
5 Please don't switch off the lights because I'm afraid of _____ .
6 I never go to the reptile house in the zoo because I'm afraid of _____ .

Total: 5

-ed and -ing adjective endings

2 Circle the correct options.
1 She is **terrified** / terrifying.
2 The film is **terrified** / terrifying. 
3 The football match is **excited** / exciting.
4 They are **excited** / exciting. 
5 He is **worried** / worrying.
6 The results are **worried** / worrying. 
7 She is **tired** / tiring.
8 The walk was **tired** / tiring.

Total: 7

Language focus
be going to / will / Present continuous

3 Read the conversation. Choose the correct options.

> A: When ¹**are you leaving** / will you leave for Japan?
> B: We ²'re leaving / 'll leave on Monday. We ³'re flying / 'll fly direct to Tokyo. We ⁴'re going to look round / 're looking round Tokyo for a few days and then we ⁵'re driving / 'll drive to Kyoto for two days.
> A: Sounds wonderful! You ⁶won't be / 're not going to be bored.
> B: Japan is beautiful. It ⁷'ll be / 's being interesting to see the temples in Kyoto.
> A: When ⁸are you coming / are you going to come back?
> B: On Sunday. We ⁹won't stay / 're not staying long.

Total: 8

Quantifiers

4 Circle the correct options.
I didn't enjoy my friend's birthday party last weekend. There were too ¹much / **many** people, there wasn't ²enough / many food and there weren't ³a little / many drinks. There weren't ⁴any / some chairs either, so we couldn't sit down. There was too ⁵many / much noise and I couldn't hear what people were saying. However, I ate ⁶a lot of / a few ice cream and then I felt better. I don't go to ⁷some / many parties because I think they're stressful!

Total: 6

a little / a few

5 Complete the sentences. Use *a little* or *a few*.
1 There are only ___a few___ biscuits left, so don't take them all!
2 I'm going to invite _____ friends to my party on Saturday.
3 There are _____ people in my class who are afraid of spiders.
4 It's OK to eat _____ sugar every day, but not too much!
5 My bedroom looks boring. I think I'll put _____ pictures on the wall.
6 Her sister is six, so she only gets _____ homework every day.

Total: 5

UNIT 6

Language builder

6 Complete the conversation with the missing words. Circle the correct options.

Josh: Let's go to the park! I ¹___ football with some friends.
Justin: Oh sorry … I ²___ my homework yet. ³___ your homework already?
Josh: Yes, I ⁴___ it yesterday! Why don't you join us later?
Justin: I haven't played football ⁵___ ages, I just don't have ⁶___ time. Our teacher gives us ⁷___ homework and then I ⁸___ study for a test on Mondays, too.
Josh: You ⁹___ worry so much. You ¹⁰___ to relax and have fun sometimes!
Justin: Yes, but if I ¹¹___ well this year, my parents ¹²___ me go to summer camp!

	a	b	c
1	play	**(b)** 'm going to play	played
2	finished	've finished	haven't finished
3	You have done	Did you do	Have you done
4	finished	have finished	finish
5	on	for	since
6	many	little	enough
7	too much	too many	a lot
8	usually have to	have to usually	have usually to
9	have to	shouldn't	don't
10	have	should	must
11	don't do	won't do	will do
12	don't let	let	won't let

Total: 11

Vocabulary builder

7 Circle the correct options.

1 I'm not climbing up there. I'm afraid of ___ .
   a lifts   **(b)** heights   c high
2 I'm worried ___ the exam tomorrow.
   a of   b about   c with
3 He scored two goals in the match and he was ___ about it for a week!
   a boasting   b criticizing   c whispering
4 I'm going to try my new contact ___ today.
   a kit   b lessons   c lenses
5 I love ___ photos.
   a taking   b making   c doing
6 I'm really tired. I'm going to ___ early tonight.
   a go to the bed   b go to a bed   c go to bed
7 I didn't like the film at all. I thought it was really ___ .
   a bored   b boring   c bore
8 Jenny's idea is not silly at all. I think it's very ___ .
   a safe   b successful   c sensible
9 Can you share that video ___ your friends on Facebook?
   a about   b with   c to
10 We're going to a theme park tomorrow. I'm really ___ .
   a exciting   b embarrassed   c excited

Total: 9

Speaking

8 Complete the conversation with the words in the box.

| serious | true | joking | way |
| impossible | ~~what~~ | believe | |

A: Have you heard? Sam's going to climb Mount Everest.
B: ¹ _What_ ? Are you ² _____ ?
A: Yes, I am. He's in a mountain climbing team.
B: That's ³ _____ . Sam's afraid of heights.
A: Imagine – he could be the youngest person to climb Everest.
B: You're ⁴ _____ !
A: No, I'm not. It's really ⁵ _____ .
B: I don't ⁶ _____ you! That's incredible!
A: They're leaving next week.
B: No ⁷ _____ ! He didn't tell me about it.

Total: 6

Total: 57

Unit 6 Review 65

Get it right! Unit 6

be going to/will/Present continuous

Remember that:
- we use *be going to* to talk about future intentions
  - ✓ *I'm going to study on Saturday night.*
  - ✗ *I will study on Saturday night.*
- we use *will* to talk about predictions in the future
  - ✓ *If I can, I will call you tomorrow.*
  - ✗ *If I can, I'm going to call you tomorrow.*
- we use the present continuous to talk about future arrangements when they have a fixed date or time
  - ✓ *I'm meeting my friends at 6 o'clock.*
  - ✗ *I'm going to meet my friends at 6 o'clock.*

1 Circle the correct words.

Jim: My dad's got a new job. My family ¹**are going to move** / will move to a new town.
Peter: No way! When are you leaving?
Jim: We ² will find / are finding out soon.
Peter: But where ³ are you going to live / are you living?
Jim: I don't know! My dad ⁴ is having / will have a meeting with his boss tomorrow. He ⁵ is going to call / is calling us as soon as he knows. Then we ⁶ will decide / are deciding where to live.

Quantifiers

Remember that:
- We use *(not) many* and *a few* with plural countable nouns
  - ✓ *There were too many people on the plane.*
  - ✗ *There were too much people on the plane.*
  - ✓ *We took a few photos at the theme park.*
  - ✗ *We took a little photos at the theme park.*
- We use *(not) much* and *a little* with uncountable nouns
  - ✓ *We spent too much money at the theme park.*
  - ✗ *We spent too many money at the theme park.*
  - ✓ *We've got a little time before the bus comes.*
  - ✗ *We've got a few time before the bus comes.*

2 Circle the correct words.
1 How **much** / many time do you spend on homework?
2 Did you take much / many photos on holiday?
3 We had a little / a few money left, so we bought ice creams.
4 There wasn't much / many food at the party.
5 There were too much / many cars in the city.
6 How much / many people came to the match?

Prepositional phrases

Remember that:
- We use *of* after *afraid, frightened, scared, terrified*:
  - ✓ *Everybody's afraid of something.*
  - ✗ *Everybody's afraid from something.*
- We use *about* after *worried, embarrassed* and *excited*:
  - ✓ *I'm really worried about my exams.*
  - ✗ *I'm really worried for my exams.*
- We use *in* after *interested*:
  - ✓ *Everyone was interested in the article.*
  - ✗ *Everyone was interested of the article.*

3 Find and correct five more mistakes with prepositional phrases in the text.

Everyone I know has something they are worried ^about ~~for~~! My mum is frightened for spiders. My sister Jane is scared for flying. My cousin Sally is excited about her school trip, but she's anxious of travelling. My dog, Bob, is terrified about storms! And me? I am very interested on phobias!

-ed and -ing adjectives

Remember that:
- We use adjectives ending with *-ed/-ied* to describe how people feel
  - ✓ *I am very interested in phobias.*
  - ✗ *I am very interesting in phobias.*
- We use adjectives ending with *-ing/-ying* to describe how things make us feel
  - ✓ *I think phobias are very interesting.*
  - ✗ *I think phobias are very interested.*
- Only people and animals can be *interested, excited, tired,* etc.

4 Add -ed/ied or -ing/ying to the adjectives.
1 Scarlett Johansson is frighten _ed_ of spiders.
2 He's really worr _____ about his exam.
3 We had a relax _____ afternoon at the beach.
4 They're excit _____ about their trip to Brazil.
5 The roller coaster was really terrif _____ .
6 My brother thinks theme parks are bor _____ .

7 School life

Vocabulary

Life at school

1 ★ Use the clues to complete the crossword.

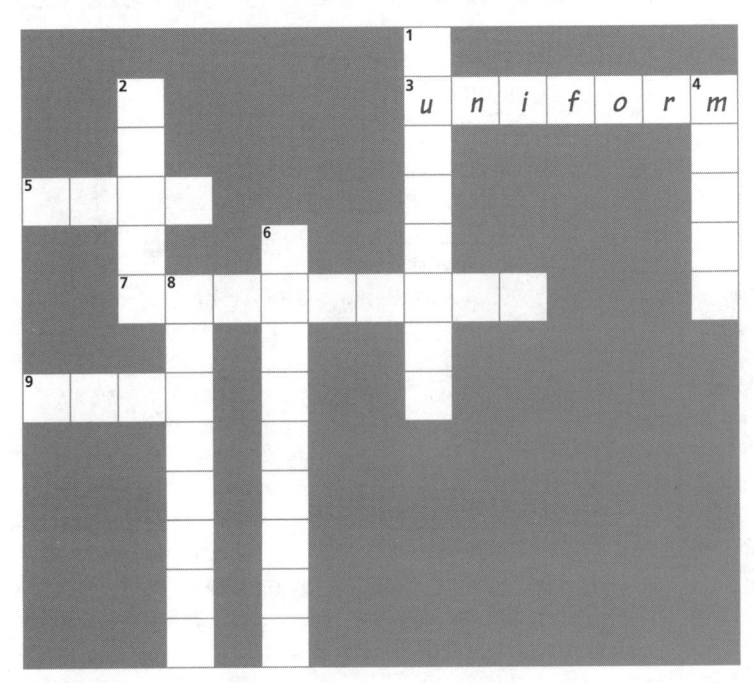

Across

3 I hate wearing a _____ . I want to wear my own clothes to school.
5 My Science teacher gets angry if we don't _____ in our homework on time.
7 We couldn't hear the teacher because there was _____ and shouting in the classroom.
9 Our Maths teacher tells us to sit at the back of the class if we don't arrive on _____ .

Down

1 Now that Ivan is doing karate the _____ from his classmates has stopped.
2 I had to write _____ after school, so I was late home again.
4 Dad always says it's important to get good _____ at school, but my gran says it's also important to have fun!
6 I can't believe you got _____ for dropping your book on the floor!
8 Most students are really good at _____ in a test, so you never see them do it.

2 ★★ Write the -ing form of words and phrases from Exercise 1.

1 Bart Simpson does this a lot!
   writing lines
2 Writing things on your arm before an exam is a way to do this.
   _____
3 We hate this because we have to stay after school. _____
4 My school starts at 8 o'clock in the morning, so this is hard for me.
   _____
5 Noisy students often do this in class.
   _____
6 If you study hard, you'll keep on doing this. _____

3 ★★ Complete the text. Use the correct form of the phrases from Exercise 1.

My granddad was telling me about his school the other day. It was very strict, and if they didn't ¹ _wear a uniform_ they had to go home and change their clothes. Students got ² _____ for things like not sitting properly in class. He said he often had to ³ _____ , usually 'I must not talk in class'. There were physical punishments, too, if you didn't arrive ⁴ _____ for school, or ⁵ _____ in an exam. Even if a teacher heard you ⁶ _____ , you had to go and see the principal. He also said there was a lot of ⁷ _____ , but no-one told the teachers. What about rewards? I asked. He said the students who always handed in ⁸ _____ the next day and got ⁹ _____ in their exams sometimes got a boring book at the end of the year. His school was very different from ours!

4 ★★★ How similar is your school to the school in Exercise 3? Which rewards and punishments do you think are the most effective? Write at least five sentences.

Unit 7   67

Language focus 1

Second conditional

1 ★ **Match the sentence halves.**
1. If I got detention, _d_
2. He wouldn't get good marks ___
3. If students had to write lines at my school, ___
4. They wouldn't get detention ___
5. If you went to school in England, ___

a if they did their homework.
b you'd have to wear a uniform.
c if he didn't cheat in tests.
d I wouldn't be able to go to my piano lesson.
e they'd probably behave better.

2 ★★ **Complete the sentences about a school in Singapore. Use the correct form of the verbs in brackets.**

1. If you _went_ (go) to this school, you _'d start_ (start) at 7.35 in the morning.
2. All the lessons _____ (be) in English if you _____ (study) there.
3. You _____ (not be) allowed to wear earrings if you _____ (be) a boy.
4. If a girl _____ (break) the rules, she _____ (get) detention.
5. If a boy or a girl _____ (not wear) their uniform, the school _____ (send) them home.
6. If a student _____ (not get) good marks, he or she _____ (go) to an after-school homework club.

3 ★★ **Complete the conversation with the second conditional. Use the verbs in the box.**

| be give ask not spend |
| help improve live go |

A: Oh dear, I failed the Maths exam! I hate Maths! If I ¹ _were_ better at it, I ² _____ hours every week on my homework. It's frustrating!
B: What about your teacher? She ³ _____ you if you ⁴ _____ her, I'm sure.
A: Maybe but she's very strict. My mum wants me to have a Maths tutor. She thinks if a tutor ⁵ _____ me extra lessons, it ⁶ _____ my marks.
B: She's probably right. Do you know, if we ⁷ _____ in Singapore, we ⁸ _____ to an after-school homework club every night? Most teenagers there do.
A: Every night? How awful!

4 ★★★ **Complete the sentences with your own ideas.**
1. It would be amazing if… _I got the best mark in the class for my test._
2. I wouldn't wear a uniform if… _____
3. I wouldn't complain if… _____
4. I would be worried if… _____
5. I would cheat in a test if… _____
6. I would have more time to do what I wanted if… _____

5 ★★★ **Imagine you were the head teacher at your school. What would you change? Write at least five sentences.**

68 Unit 7

Listening and vocabulary

Listening

1 ★ 🔊 07 **Listen to Kesia talking to her dad about her education. What does she want to do? Does her dad agree?**

2 ★★ 🔊 07 **Read the sentences. Listen again and circle the correct options.**
1 Kesia is **14** / **16** years old.
2 She says she **never has fun** / **doesn't like the rules** at school.
3 She thinks she'd learn **more** / **less** if she didn't go to school.
4 She found out about home education from **the Internet** / **her friends**.
5 Her dad thinks home education would be **easy** / **difficult** to organise.
6 With home education you **can** / **can't** study outside the classroom.
7 Kesia **would** / **wouldn't** be able to see her friends if she's not at school.
8 Kesia **often** / **never** does homework with her friends.
9 Kesia's dad decides **he will talk to her mother** / **she should leave school now**.
10 Kesia needs to find out more about **home education** / **university**.

make and do

3 ★ **Complete the phrases with make or do.**
1 _make_ friends
2 _____ your homework
3 _____ something interesting
4 _____ a phone call
5 _____ a mess
6 _____ decisions
7 _____ the right thing
8 _____ a mistake
9 _____ an exercise
10 _____ a noise

4 ★★ **Complete the sentences with the phrases in Exercise 3.**
1 You have to _do your homework_ or you can't go to the party.
2 I hate shopping with Liam. It's impossible for him to _____ about what to buy.
3 Can you wait for a minute? I just need to _____ to a friend.
4 It's really easy for Sue to _____ . She knows everyone!
5 I did the wrong homework! I always _____ when I copy from the board!
6 Do you think I should buy Annie a present to say thank you for helping me? I want to _____ .
7 Look at the kitchen! Why do you always _____ when you cook?
8 Let's _____ this weekend, like watching horror films at your house.

Unit 7   69

Language focus 2

Second conditional questions

1 ★★ **Put the words in the correct order to make questions.**

1 at / you / they / prize / you / school, / If / what / won / a / give / would / ?
If you won a prize at school, what would they give you?

2 you / if / your / detention / tell / you / got / parents / Would / ?
_____
_____

3 If / you / be / rule, / change / would / school / one / could / it / what / ?
_____
_____

4 you / another / friends / Would / went / if / make / quickly / to / you / school?
_____
_____

5 you / decision, / make / an / talk / wanted / to / If / important / you / who / would / to / ?
_____
_____

6 would / your / fun / do / If / friends / something / tonight, / what / did / they / ?
_____
_____

2 ★ **Match the answers with the questions in Exercise 1.**

a We'd start class at 11 o'clock, not 8 o'clock!
b They'd probably go skateboarding.
c No, I wouldn't.
d They'd give me a book and a certificate.
e Yes, I would. I'm quite sociable.
f I would probably talk to my sister.

1 *d*
2 __
3 __
4 __
5 __
6 __

3 ★★ **Complete the conversation. Use the correct form of the verbs in brackets or a short answer.**

A: What kind of teacher ¹ *would you be* (you be)?
B: What do you mean?
A: Well, if ² _____ (you be) a teacher, ³ _____ (you be) strict?
B: No, I ⁴ _____ – definitely not! I prefer teachers who don't punish you.
A: Well, I'm not sure. What ⁵ _____ (you do) if ⁶ _____ (the students not listen to you)?
B: I don't know. ⁷ _____ (you give) detention?
A: Probably. ⁸ _____ (the students respect) you less if ⁹ _____ (you not give) them detention?
B: Maybe, yes. But really, ¹⁰ _____ (you want) to be a teacher?
A: Yes, ¹¹ _____ . I think I'd enjoy it.
B: Oh! What ¹² _____ (you teach) then?
A: Physics, probably.

4 ★★★ **Imagine you are home educated. Write the questions. Then answer them for you.**

what / study?   do exams?   where / go?
what / be the best thing about it?
miss anything at school?

If you were home educated, … *what would you study? I'd probably study Geography, History and …*

Explore phrasal verbs (3)

5 ★★ **Circle the correct options.**

1 I wrote off / **out** all the names carefully before I made a decision.
2 Would you like to try **out** / **on** our new computer software?
3 Small children pick **out** / **up** a lot of new words from their parents.
4 I spent hours thinking about it but I couldn't work **out** / **off** the answer.
5 The teacher found **out** / **off** they were cheating because they had the same answers.

Reading

1 ★ Read Ted's text about an experiment at his school. What is a 'secret student'? Did it work at Ted's school?

'SECRET STUDENT'
You might be the 'SECRET STUDENT' today!

Last year my school tried a new way to get students to **behave** better in class. It's called the 'secret student', and the idea is not to punish bad behaviour but reward good behaviour *instead*. If your class gets enough points, they get a prize at the end of the year.

Here's what happens. Every morning the class teacher chooses a secret student **at random** – by picking a name from a box. This person represents the class all day. In every lesson the teacher monitors him or her, and gives a tick for good behaviour or a cross for bad behaviour. At the end of the day, the *class* is awarded a point if the secret student has got more ticks than crosses. The **crucial** thing about this system is that if you were the secret student you wouldn't know, so everyone has to behave well to make sure the class gets a point. The teachers only **reveal** the identity of that day's secret student if they award a point, but if the student doesn't get a point their identity stays secret.

The idea of the secret student is to make everyone feel their behaviour has consequences for the whole class, not just for them individually. It also means students **encourage** each other to behave: 'You could be the secret student, stop talking!' The teachers also **warn** students who start behaving badly: 'Jan, you might be the secret student! Do you want a tick? Then sit down!' In the end everybody becomes more responsible, and it brings the class together.

It certainly worked in my class. Our behaviour was much better and we got 108 points, which was enough for a day at a theme park after our exams. We had an amazing time, so it was definitely **worth it**!

Secret Student — Tuesday 25 April
Henry Clyde

Class	Behaviour
1	✓
2	✗
3	✓
4	✓
5	✓
6	✗

2 ★★ Complete the sentences with the words in *bold* from the text.
1 My parents always __encourage__ me to try lots of different activities.
2 I must _____ you. If I see anyone cheating, they will get a zero!
3 If you can't come tomorrow, you can come on Thursday _____.
4 I had to train really hard all winter but it was _____. I won a silver medal!
5 They choose the numbers in the Christmas lottery _____.
6 Next week they will _____ the winners of the short story competition.
7 Polly, stop hitting Peter! If you don't _____, you won't go to the circus.
8 The expert said that lots of practice is _____ if you want to get better.

3 ★★ Read the text again. Are these sentences true (*T*) or false (*F*)? Correct the false sentences.
1 Ted's school has used this method for five years. *F*
   They started it last year.
2 The method rewards students for good behaviour.
   _____
3 One student represents all the students in the class.
   _____
4 Each lesson has a different secret student.
   _____
5 The teachers give points for every lesson.
   _____
6 Only one person knows who the secret student is.
   _____
7 The students try to make sure everyone behaves.
   _____
8 If you get enough points, you can do something fun.
   _____

4 ★★★ What do you think of the 'secret student' idea? Do you think it would work with your class? What would happen? Write your ideas.

Writing

A problem page

1 Read the advice leaflet. Who is it for?

HOW TO MAKE FRIENDS AT A NEW SCHOOL!

It's hard to change schools and leave all your friends. The problem is that in a new school everything is different. You even get lost going to your classroom! So if you're at a new school, how can you make friends fast?

- The most important thing is you **¹ can / (must)** be yourself – don't try to change your personality to suit other people. When people discover your personality, they will accept you.

- **² Think carefully / Make sure** about making a good impression. You **³ never / should** dress in clothes you feel comfortable in but nothing too extreme!

- **⁴ Never / Make sure** sit alone at the back of the class. Always try to sit with other people in class or in the canteen.

- You might be nervous, but **⁵ don't / make sure** you're nice to people, and **⁶ don't / think carefully** be rude. Keep smiling and try to look interested.

- If you see someone else on their own, you **⁷ don't / should** go and talk to them. They might be new at the school too and need a friend!

- You **⁸ could also / also could** try to get involved with activities and join after-school clubs. You might find people who are interested in doing the same things as you.

Stay positive and you'll soon make friends!

2 Read the advice leaflet again. Circle the correct options.

3 Read the leaflet again. Match the questions with the answers.
1 What's the problem with starting a new school?   _d_   a A positive one.
2 Why shouldn't you change your personality?   ___   b They are also alone.
3 Where shouldn't you sit?   ___   c Join activities and go to after-school clubs.
4 How should you behave?   ___   d Everything is new.
5 What kind of attitude is best?   ___   e Smile and be nice.
6 What's the best way to look?   ___   f People will accept the way you are.
7 How can you recognise another new student?   ___   g On your own at the back of the class.
8 How can you meet people with the same interests?   ___   h Like you are interested.

Writing

Useful language — Summarising a problem and giving advice

4 Complete the sentences with the words in the box.

> tell ~~also~~ really say could possible

1 The problem is not only that you feel stress but ____*also*____ that it affects your health.
2 It's _____ that you're trying to do too much.
3 I think you should _____ the truth.
4 You _____ that you can't relax but you have to.
5 You _____ also tell your teacher.
6 I _____ hope this helps.

5 Match the sentence halves.

1 If you are feeling stressed,   *c*
2 If you're not sleeping well,   ___
3 If you can't study,   ___
4 If you've got exams,   ___
5 If there's bullying in your school,   ___

a keep trying to do a bit every day.
b tell your teacher or the principal.
c take deep breaths and relax.
d do more exercise – but not before you go to bed!
e don't leave your studying to the last minute.

> **WRITING TIP**
> Make it better! ✓ ✓ ✓
> We always use the *-ing* form of a verb after a preposition.

6 Choose the correct options.

1 It's hard (to concentrate) / concentrating sometimes.
2 Keep on **to try / trying** even if you fail.
3 Think about **to change / changing** your diet.
4 If you're not interested in **to do / doing** an activity, don't do it!
5 Try to **keep / keeping** your bedroom tidy.

> **WRITING TIP**
> Make it better! ✓ ✓ ✓
> End the leaflet with something positive.

7 Read the sentences. Which one is <u>not</u> positive?
1 Stay happy and don't give up.
2 Don't forget: you can do it!
3 Believe in yourself and you'll do it!
4 Remember these rules.

8 Number the things in the list in the order they appear in the advice leaflet.

a final sentence to make people feel positive ___
who the leaflet is for, and a question for them ___
a title   *1*
several tips (pieces of advice) ___
an explanation of the problem ___

PLAN

9 You are going to write an advice leaflet about how to avoid stress at school. Make notes about the things in Exercise 8.

WRITE

10 Write your advice leaflet. Look at page 83 of the Student's Book to help you.

_____
_____
_____
_____
_____
_____
_____
_____
_____
_____
_____
_____
_____
_____
_____
_____

CHECK

11 Check your writing. Can you say YES to these questions?
- Is the information in Exercise 8 in your leaflet?
- Have you introduced the advice with different expressions?
- Have you used conditionals in your writing?
- Are the *-ing* verbs and infinitives correct?
- Does the leaflet end with a positive message?
- Are the spelling and punctuation correct?

Do you need to write a second draft?

7 Review

Vocabulary
Life at school

1 Complete the sentences with the words in box.

> detention bullying marks cheating
> ~~uniform~~ time shout lines

1 We can wear jeans and T-shirts to school – we don't have to wear a ____uniform____ .
2 Dave didn't do his homework and so he got _____ .
3 Students get good _____ if they show they've worked hard.
4 You can't copy from another student – that's _____ .
5 You mustn't _____ at your classmates – it's very rude.
6 Sometimes we have to write _____ when we behave badly.
7 Cindy is always late for class. She has problems being on _____ .
8 You shouldn't be aggressive with students that are younger than you – that's _____ .

☐ Total: 7

make and *do*

2 Complete the table with the words in the box.

> homework   a decision   phone calls
> something fun   ~~friends~~   a mistake
> the right thing   a mess   an exercise   a noise

Make	Do
friends	

☐ Total: 9

Language focus
Second conditional

3 (Circle) the correct options.
1 If you **would study** / **(studied)** harder, you **(would get)** / **got** better marks in your tests.
2 He **wouldn't get** / **didn't get** so many detentions, if he **would be** / **was** on time.
3 If the teacher **would see** / **saw** you cheating, she **wouldn't give** / **didn't give** you good marks.
4 We **would have** / **had** more free time if we **wouldn't have** / **didn't have** so much homework.
5 If I **would be** / **was** a bit taller, I **would be** / **was** on the school netball team.
6 She **would be** / **was** lonely if she **wouldn't go** / **didn't go** to school.

☐ Total: 5

Second conditional questions

4 Complete the second conditional questions. Use *you* and the correct form of the verbs in brackets.
1 What ____would you say____ (say) if ____you met____ (meet) your favourite musician?
2 If _____ (have) a car, where _____ (go)?
3 What _____ (do) if _____ (not have to) go to school?
4 If _____ (win) the lottery, _____ (spend) all the money immediately?
5 _____ (fly) to the Moon if _____ (have) enough money?
6 If _____ (not pass) an exam, what _____ (say) to your parents?

☐ Total: 5

UNIT 7

Language builder

5 Complete the conversation with the missing words. Circle the correct options.

> **Sally:** ¹___ on time for school?
> **Julie:** Yes. I ²___ late this term yet!
> **Sally:** I've been late three times ³___ , and I ⁴___ detention last week.
> **Julie:** That's not good. ⁵___ play in the school football team this year?
> **Sally:** I probably ⁶___ because I've got ⁷___ work to do. I ⁸___ the team if I ⁹___ exams at the end of this year. How about you?
> **Julie:** I ¹⁰___ yet. I ¹¹___ join the tennis team. The problem is there aren't many tennis courts at school.
> **Sally:** If you ¹²___ to school early, you'd get a place on a court easily!

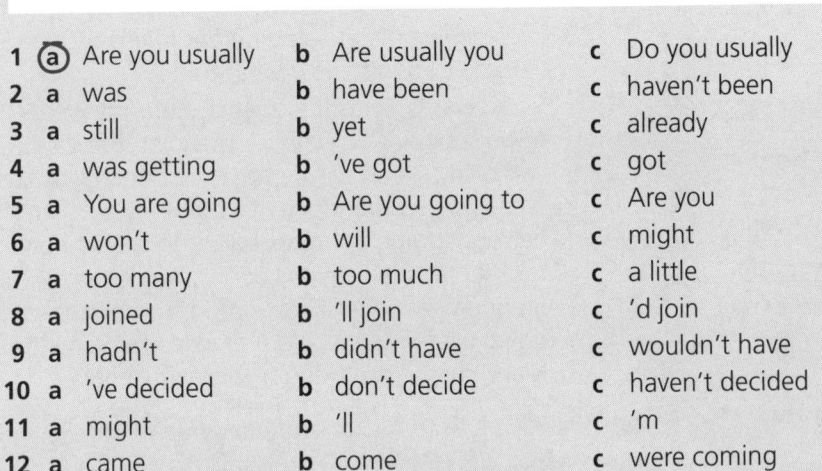

1. **a** Are you usually   **b** Are usually you   **c** Do you usually
2. **a** was   **b** have been   **c** haven't been
3. **a** still   **b** yet   **c** already
4. **a** was getting   **b** 've got   **c** got
5. **a** You are going   **b** Are you going to   **c** Are you
6. **a** won't   **b** will   **c** might
7. **a** too many   **b** too much   **c** a little
8. **a** joined   **b** 'll join   **c** 'd join
9. **a** hadn't   **b** didn't have   **c** wouldn't have
10. **a** 've decided   **b** don't decide   **c** haven't decided
11. **a** might   **b** 'll   **c** 'm
12. **a** came   **b** come   **c** were coming

Total: 11

Vocabulary builder

6 Circle the correct options.
1. You've ___ a real mess of your homework. Do it again!
   a done   **b** made   **c** had
2. The school rules are clear. You must be ___ time every day.
   a at   **b** of   **c** on
3. Vicki doesn't seem very worried ___ getting detention.
   a of   **b** about   **c** with
4. If you ___ a cold, you'll miss the big match on Saturday.
   a catch   **b** take   **c** make
5. If I had more time, I'd ___ with my friends more.
   a keep on   **b** set up   **c** hang out
6. You should ___ the right thing and tell the teacher.
   a do   **b** make   **c** have
7. Please ___ your homework on Monday.
   a go up   **b** try out   **c** hand in
8. She can't sleep. She's afraid of ___ .
   a the dark   **b** dark   **c** a dark
9. It's ___ today. I'm so cold!
   a freezing   **b** heat wave   **c** snowstorm
10. At the market there was a ___ throwing ten balls in the air!
    a busker   **b** juggler   **c** mural

Total: 9

Speaking

7 Put the sentences in the correct order to make a conversation asking for and giving advice.
___ **Julie:** Have you tried talking to your parents?
___ **Julie:** Oh dear. If I were you, I'd talk to the teacher about it.
___ **Julie:** What's the problem?
_1_ **Zoe:** Hi Julie! I need your advice.
___ **Zoe:** I can't finish all my homework. What do you think I should do?
___ **Zoe:** I can't do that. She'll think I'm lazy!
___ **Zoe:** Yes, maybe that's the best idea.

Total: 6

Total: 52

Unit 7 Review 75

Get it right! Unit 7

Second conditional

Remember that:
- we use *if* + subject + the past simple in the action/situation clause
  ✓ *If I knew the answer, I would tell you.*
- we use *would/wouldn't* + infinitive to talk about the consequences of the action/situation.
  ✓ *If I knew the answer, I would tell you.*
- We don't use *will* to talk about the consequences of the action/situation
  ✗ *If I knew the answer, I will tell you.*
- We don't use *would/wouldn't* + infinitive in the same clause as *if*.
  ✗ *If I would know, I would tell you.*

1 Are the sentences correct? Correct the incorrect sentences.
1. If I would go to England, I would visit Cambridge.
   If I went to England, I would visit Cambridge.
2. They will be very happy if they went to a Free School.
   _____
3. If I had the choice, I would go on holiday.
   _____
4. I won't go to bed early if it would be the holidays.
   _____

Second conditional questions

Remember that:
We form questions about the results of imaginary situations using *would(n't)* + subject + verb. The subject comes between *would(n't)* and the main verb.
✓ *What would you do if you saw someone cheating?*
✗ *What you would do if you saw someone cheating?*
✓ *If you saw someone cheating, what would you do?*
✗ *If you saw someone cheating, what you would do?*

2 Complete the second conditional questions with *would* and the words in brackets.
1. *What would your parents do* (do / your parents / what) if you were unhappy at school?
2. _____ (go / they) to a Free School if they had the choice?
3. If you could live anywhere, _____ (live / you / where)?
4. _____ (buy / you / what) if you had a million pounds?

want, *choose* and *decide*

Remember that:
We use the infinitive with *to* after *want*, *choose*, and *decide*
✓ *I don't want to do the exam tomorrow.*
✗ *I don't want do the exam tomorrow.*
✗ *I don't want doing the exam tomorrow.*

3 Find and correct seven more mistakes with *want*, *choose* and *decide* in the text.

Everyone wants ~~doing~~ *to do* different things on Saturday. I don't know what to do! Sarah wants go to the cinema, but Amy wants to go shopping. If I choose spending the day with Amy, Sarah will be upset. My mum and dad want visit my grandparents, but if my brother decides staying at home, I want to stay at home, too! If I tell my parents I don't want visit my grandparents, they'll be angry. If I could choose doing anything, I would play videogames with Mark, but he can't decide what do either!

make and *do*

Remember that:
- We use *do* with nouns for activities
  ✓ *We often do a quiz in class.*
  ✗ *We often make a quiz in class.*
  ✓ *I usually do my homework on Sunday.*
  ✗ *I usually make my homework on Sunday.*
- We use *make* with nouns when we create or produce something new
  ✓ *I made a lot of mistakes in the exam.*
  ✗ *I did a lot of mistakes in the exam.*
  ✓ *You should make a list of your ideas.*
  ✗ *You should do a list of your ideas.*

4 Complete the sentences with the correct form of *do* or *make*.
1. She's ___*made*___ a lot of new friends at school.
2. I couldn't hear because my brother was _____ too much noise.
3. You would sleep better if you _____ more exercise.
4. Did you _____ anything interesting at the weekend?
5. You've _____ such a mess in your room!
6. Do you like _____ sports at your school?

8 Green planet

Vocabulary

Materials

1 ★ Find ten words for materials in the wordsquare.

p	m	e	t	a	l	g	b	o	s	a	p
r	e	t	h	v	m	a	r	o	h	p	l
o	t	l	e	a	t	h	e	r	a	z	a
c	b	q	u	a	l	b	z	p	v	o	s
e	l	r	c	a	r	h	e	m	p	w	t
m	e	m	i	t	o	r	n	r	o	l	i
e	g	g	r	c	c	r	k	o	c	e	c
n	u	l	b	i	k	u	d	n	o	a	y
t	y	a	a	p	l	s	o	f	t	n	e
a	w	f	u	s	w	i	s	a	t	e	l
l	a	c	k	i	s	t	r	e	o	b	l
k	r	u	b	b	e	r	q	a	n	d	o

2 ★ Complete the sentences. Use the first letter to help you.
1. Put on those yellow r _ubber gloves_ if you're going to wash the dishes.
2. This table is made of w_____ from a sustainable forest.
3. He's allergic to artificial fibres, so he usually wears clothes made from pure organic c_____ .
4. Vegans don't eat or use animal products, so they don't wear l_____ jackets or shoes.
5. The ancient Egyptians wrote on papyrus but the Chinese invented p_____ in about 200 BC.
6. Gold is not the most expensive m_____ in the world. Platinum and rhodium cost more.
7. The ancient Romans used b_____ and c_____ for many of their buildings.
8. In a lot of discos people drink out of p_____ glasses, because g_____ ones could break.

3 ★★ Match the materials in Exercise 1 with the objects.
1. houses, fireplaces, walls _bricks_
2. sofas, belts, shoes _____
3. floors, stairs, plant pots _____
4. saxophones, spoons, cans _____
5. toys, pens, bottles _____
6. windows, mirrors, bottles _____
7. notebooks, cards, boxes _____
8. car tyres, children's balls, kitchen gloves _____
9. pencils, cupboards, tables _____
10. T-shirts, jeans, rugs _____

4 ★★ Complete the text about Sue's living room.

This picture is our new living room. Mum and Dad have made big changes! The floor is ¹ _wood_ with lots of rugs, and one wall and the fireplace are now the original ² _____ . The other walls have got ³ _____ with tree designs painted by hand. The old sofa has gone and now we've got a fantastic ⁴ _____ one. The windows have got beautiful green ⁵ _____ curtains. The new dining table is very modern. It's got a ⁶ _____ top with ⁷ _____ legs. Honestly, it could be out of a magazine! The only horrible thing is that cheap ⁸ _____ model of a spaceship I made when I was six. My mum loves it and keeps it on the TV!

5 ★★★ Find objects in your bedroom for the materials. Write the names of the objects and the materials. Use a dictionary if necessary. Can you find all ten materials?

Object name   Material(s)
photo frame   _metal, glass and plastic_

Unit 8   77

Language focus 1

Present simple passive

1 ★ **Match the sentence halves.**
1. The metal rhodium is — _f_
2. Old tyres are — __
3. Plastic bags are — __
4. Modern bricks are — __
5. New houses are — __
6. Car windows are — __
7. Small amounts of gold are — __

a made from plastic and glass.
b recycled for artificial football pitches.
c built to be more energy-efficient.
d found in the stomachs of whales.
e used to make mobile phones.
f found in South Africa.
g heated to high temperatures before use in buildings.

2 ★★ **Write passive sentences with the prompts.**

1. Most glass / produce / in big factories
   Most glass is produced in big factories.
2. Glass / make / with sand and other minerals
   _____
3. They / melt together / at 1700 °C
   _____
4. Other materials / add / to produce different colours
   _____
5. Glass / use / in many important industries
   _____
6. Before glass / recycle / it / separate / into different colours
   _____
7. When glass / recycle / no material / lose
   _____

3 ★★ **Complete the text with the active or passive form of the verbs in brackets.**

Because most people ¹ ___replace___ (replace) their mobile phone every two years or less, about 125 million phones ² _____ (throw) in the bin every year in the USA. The problem is that many mobiles ³ _____ (contain) dangerous metals, like lead, mercury and cadmium, so if they ⁴ _____ (throw) away they ⁵ _____ (pollute) the environment. Now, organisations like 'Call2Recycle' ⁶ _____ (offer) to take your old phone for recycling. Your old phone ⁷ _____ (collect), and then it ⁸ _____ (sell) back to the company that made it. Then either it ⁹ _____ (sell) again in another country, or it ¹⁰ _____ (take) to pieces for the materials, like plastic, glass and metal, and the electronic components.

4 ★★★ **Answer the questions. Use the present simple passive.**
1. What material are the shoes you are wearing today made of?
   _____
2. What happens to your old mobile phones?
   _____
3. What does your town do about recycling?
   _____
4. What happens at your school to help the environment?
   _____
5. What happens at home?
   _____

5 ★★★ **Think about your town or city. What happens there every day? Write sentences. Use the present simple passive.**
1. _The rubbish is collected from the streets._
2. _____
3. _____
4. _____
5. _____
6. _____

Listening and vocabulary

Listening

1 ★★ 🔊 **08** Listen to a radio programme called 'Everyday problems'. What can you do with your old gadgets? What should you never do?

You can _____
or _____.
You should never _____.

2 ★★ 🔊 **08** Listen again and complete the sentences.

1 Most homes have got things they don't want, like _games consoles_ , _____, _____ and tablets.
2 Often it's because we buy new, _____, _____ versions.
3 Monica says there are _____ categories, things _____ and things _____.
4 For the first category, the options are: _____ online or _____ to charity.
5 Some _____ and _____ look for old gadgets for students.
6 When charities are given old gadgets, they are _____ and _____, or _____.
7 Electronics can contain metals like _____ and _____.
8 There are lots of companies that _____.
9 You shouldn't throw gadgets in the rubbish because they can _____.
10 The information about useful organisations is _____ the programme's _____.

Energy issues

3 ★★ Circle the correct options.

1 My dad says we need to **turn down** / **reduce** the gas we use.
2 If you want to pay less, you have to **consume** / **save** less electricity.
3 We're trying to **consume** / **save** money by **turning down** / **switching off** the water temperature in the shower.
4 Who **wastes** / **leaves on standby** the most electricity in your house?
5 My sister never **wastes** / **switches off** her computer! She often leaves it on all night.
6 When you **leave** / **reduce** the TV on standby, it's still consuming energy.

4 ★★ Complete the advice with words from Exercise 3.

Easy ways to go GREEN!

- Always ¹ _switch off_ the lights when you leave a room or before you go out.
- Don't leave your electronic devices on ² _____ when you go to sleep. All those little red or green lights ³ _____ more energy than you think!
- Don't ⁴ _____ water. Have shorter showers, and when you brush your teeth don't use water until the end.
- ⁵ _____ how much meat you eat by going vegetarian one day a week.
- ⁶ _____ the heating and put on a jumper.
- ⁷ _____ plastic bags and bottles so you can use them again.

Language focus 2

Past simple passive

1 ★ **Complete the sentences with the past simple passive. Add *by* where necessary.**
  1 In Ancient China windows __were made of__ paper because they didn't have glass. (make)
  2 Cave paintings show that leather clothing _____ people who lived 12,000 years ago. (wear)
  3 The World Wide Web _____ until the 1990s. (not develop)
  4 The first rubber boots _____ in France in 1853. (produce)
  5 The potato came to Europe from Peru. It _____ Spanish sailors. (bring)
  6 The first lightbulb _____ Edison, but he got the money. (not invent)
  7 The first rules of football _____ (write down) in Cambridge in 1848.

Past simple passive questions

2 ★★ **Write past simple passive questions about these important discoveries. Then match the questions with the answers.**
  1 When / X-rays / discover?
    __When were X-rays discovered?__ c
  2 Who / penicillin / discover / by / 1928?
    _____
  3 What / discover / Alfred Nobel / 1866?
    _____
  4 What / develop / Michael Faraday / 1821?
    _____
  5 When / the magnifying glass / develop?
    _____
  6 Who / the first motor car / make / by?
    _____
  7 What / make / in the 1920s / by John Logie Baird?
    _____

  a Dynamite.
  b Karl Benz, in 1886.
  c In 1895, by Wilhelm Röntgen.
  d In 1250, by Roger Bacon.
  e The television.
  f Doctor Alexander Fleming.
  g The electric motor.

3 ★★★ **Complete the text with the past simple form of the verbs in brackets.**

Q: Who [1] __was__ Greenpeace __set up__ (set up) by?
A: No-one's really sure! Lots of people contributed.
Q: When and where [2] _____ Greenpeace _____ (start)?
A: In Canada in 1971, but it [3] _____ (not call) Greenpeace at first. A group of activists went to protest against an underground nuclear explosion in Alaska. Their boat [4] _____ (stop) and the nuclear test [5] _____ (not prevent), but, because of the campaign, a few months later all nuclear activity at the island [6] _____ (end) by the US government. That was the beginning of Greenpeace.
Q: When [7] _____ Greenpeace International _____ (create)?
A: In 1979. Several Greenpeace groups in different countries [8] _____ (combine) to make one worldwide organisation. Later an office [9] _____ (open) in Amsterdam, and soon Greenpeace activists [10] _____ (find) campaigning all over the world!

4 ★★★ **What five discoveries and inventions do you think were most important for the way we live now? Write past passive sentences. Use the Internet!**

An electric current was produced by Alessandro Volta in 1800.

Explore phrasal verbs (4)

5 ★★ **Complete the sentences with the correct form of the verbs in the box.**

  bring down   keep on   put up
  ~~cut down~~   knock down

  1 A lot of trees __were cut down__ to make way for the new road.
  2 I couldn't do it the first time, but I _____ trying and I learned.
  3 They _____ a lot of houses in this street since we moved here.
  4 If we plant trees around our house, it _____ the temperature.
  5 Our old school _____ last year to build a completely new one.

Reading

1 ★ Read the text about drinks cans. Choose the correct summary.
a How you can become a millionaire selling drinks in cans.
b How recycling cans is better for the environment.
c How we can help the environment by not buying drinks in cans.

WHAT 'CAN' WE DO?

475 billion cans of drink are sold in the world every year. What happens to all these empty aluminium cans? Amazingly, a lot of them are recycled! It takes 100 years for an aluminium can to **decompose** in a **landfill**. So recycling makes sense.

Aluminium doesn't **occur** naturally. It's made from bauxite in a process called smelting. Producing aluminium is **energy-intensive**. Bauxite is extracted by **mining**, which is expensive and creates environmental problems. Bauxite mining **harms** forests, which affects plants and animals, and the chemicals which are used in the process affect the health of people living there.

Recycling reduces the need to mine bauxite. Recycling aluminium consumes only 5% of the energy needed to produce it by mining and smelting. In fact, making *one* can with recycled aluminium saves enough energy to **run** a television for three hours!

Aluminium is one of the most common materials in modern life. It's the cheapest material to recycle, and can be recycled indefinitely because it isn't damaged by the process. Cans are also one of the easiest things to recycle – new drinks cans appear in the shops only six weeks after recycling!

In some countries people pay extra for each can they buy. If they recycle the can or take it back to a shop, they get this money back. Many places have got special machines where cans are **crushed**, and you get a ticket saying how many cans you recycled so you can reclaim the money. In Sweden, where this is very successful, 92% of cans are recycled. In Britain, people sell empty cans for charity. There are several hundred places that buy cans and then recycle them. Just imagine – if every can in the UK were recycled like this, it would raise over £30 million a year for good causes!

2 ★★ Match the words in **bold** from the text with the definitions.
1 disintegrate — *decompose*
2 pushed down into a small space _____
3 exist somewhere _____
4 has a bad effect on or damages _____
5 a large place where rubbish is put in the ground _____
6 extracting minerals from the ground _____
7 give a machine the energy to work _____
8 using a lot of energy _____

3 ★★ Read the text again and answer the questions.
1 What happens to most drinks cans?
   They are recycled.
2 What is aluminium made from?
3 What two problems about mining this does the text mention?
4 Why is recycling a better alternative to mining?
5 What three advantages are there when recycling aluminium?
6 How long is the whole recycling process?
7 What happens in some countries to encourage recycling?
8 How do we know this works well in Sweden?
9 What happens in Britain?
10 Why can you make a lot of money doing this?

4 ★★★ What happens to cans in your country? Which of the ways explained in the article do you think is best? What do you think is the best way to stop people just throwing cans away? Write four or five sentences.

Unit 8

Writing

A newspaper article

1 Read Luke's article for his school newspaper. Why will he be on TV?

Last month I went to a meeting about saving water. The event was organised by a local TV channel, and afterwards my family volunteered to try to reduce the amount of water we use. 'How do we save water?' ¹ _____asked_____ my dad.

The TV company suggested easy ways to save water. 'One of them is a five-minute limit on showers,' they ² _____ . Another was to stop wasting water while we brushed our teeth. 'You only really need water at the end,' they ³ _____ . Then one day they came to our house: 'We want to film you at home!' they ⁴ _____ us.

A TV crew came to our house when we started and again yesterday. The first time they didn't film me, but this time I was filmed switching on the dishwasher! It's great. My family have used these ideas and saved water, and we'll be on TV!

2 Complete Luke's article for his school newspaper. Use the words in the box.

explained   told   ~~asked~~   said

3 Read the article again and answer the questions.
1. What was the meeting about?
   Reducing the water you use at home.
2. Who organised it?
   _____
3. What do Luke's family have to do?
   _____
4. What is the maximum time for a shower to save water?
   _____
5. When doesn't Luke need to use water?
   _____
6. How does he feel about the experience?
   _____

Useful language — Using direct speech

> **WRITING TIP**
> Make it better! ✓ ✓ ✓
> Use direct speech to show the reader exactly what someone said – it makes your writing more interesting.

4 Write these sentences in direct speech.
1. He explained that we are participating in a TV programme.
   You are participating in a TV programme.
2. He asked me how much water I use.
   _____
3. They explained that it's very easy to save water.
   _____
4. He told me it'll be on TV tomorrow.
   _____
5. They said we use too much water.
   _____

5 (Circle) the correct time linkers.
1. We went to a meeting and **after** / **(afterwards)** they told us about the programme.
2. They told us to turn off the TV **while** / **when** we went to bed.
3. **One** / **A** day, a TV crew came to my house.
4. I watched an interesting TV programme **the last week** / **last week**.
5. He'll have to do it again but **this time** / **that time** on film.

82 Unit 8

Writing

6 Complete the sentences with the active or passive form of the verbs in brackets.
1. The TV crew ___filmed___ (film) me switching off lights in the house.
2. The meeting _____ (organise) by a local TV channel.
3. They _____ (explain) different ways to save energy.
4. We _____ (ask) lots of questions about different habits.
5. They _____ (work out) how much energy we could save in a month.
6. All the videos _____ (post) online the week after the programme.

> **WRITING TIP**
> Make it better! ✓ ✓ ✓
> Give background information at the beginning of the article to explain to the reader why something happened.

7 Read the sentences. Which one does <u>not</u> give background information?
1. A TV channel sent us a letter asking if we'd like to participate in a TV programme.
2. My family and I will be on TV next month!
3. Last month I wrote to a TV channel about one of their programmes.
4. Last Sunday about 200 people went to the local TV station for an interview.
5. In March, my family found out we were going to be part of a TV programme.

8 Read the article again. Make notes about the things Luke writes about.

Who is involved	Luke, his family and a local TV channel.
What they did	
When they did it	
What happened	
What the consequences were	
What is happening next	

9 Imagine you are participating in a TV programme about saving energy. You are going to write an article about it for the school newspaper. Make notes for each heading in Exercise 8.

WRITE

10 Write your article. Look at page 93 of the Student's Book to help you.

_____
_____
_____
_____
_____
_____
_____
_____
_____
_____
_____
_____
_____
_____
_____
_____
_____

CHECK

11 Check your writing. Can you say YES to these questions?
- Is the information from the list in Exercise 8 in your article?
- Have you used direct speech in your article?
- Have you used time linkers correctly?
- Have you used the active and passive correctly?
- Have you given the reader some background information?
- Are the spelling and punctuation correct?

Do you need to write a second draft?

8 Review

Vocabulary
Materials

1 Complete the table with the words in the box.

car tyres trumpets buildings T-shirts walls
~~windows~~ toys books pencils shoes

Glass	Plastic	Metal	Bricks	Wood
windows				
Cement	**Leather**	**Cotton**	**Rubber**	**Paper**

Total: 9

Energy issues

2 Complete the text with the words in the box.

reduce ~~consume~~ turn waste
save switch leave

People ¹_consume_ large amounts of energy every day. Sometimes they ²_____ energy when they ³_____ their computers and TVs on standby all night. If you ⁴_____ down the heating and ⁵_____ off appliances when you don't need them, it will ⁶_____ your energy bills. And it helps the planet to ⁷_____ energy because there is less pollution.

Total: 6

Language focus
Present simple passive

3 Complete the text with the present passive form of the verbs in brackets.

We've got a very good recycling programme in our city – our waste ¹ _is not thrown_ (not throw away). These blue bins ² _____ (collect) once a week. They ³ _____ (use) for paper and plastic. It ⁴ _____ (recycle) to make new paper and plastic. This green bin ⁵ _____ (not collect) every week – they only empty it every two weeks. It ⁶ _____ (use) for garden rubbish, like leaves. It ⁷ _____ (recycle) to make garden fertilizer. Some things, like phones and laptops ⁸ _____ (recycle), too. However, they ⁹ _____ (not collect) by the town council.

Total: 8

Past simple passive

4 Complete the text with the past simple passive form of the verbs in brackets. Add *by* where necessary.

This eco-house ¹ _was built_ (build) in 1995. It ² _____ (design) Josie Jackman, an architect and 'eco warrior'. Solar panels ³ _____ (install) to provide all the energy for heating the house in winter. The walls ⁴ _____ (not make) from bricks, they ⁵ _____ (make) from recycled plastic and paper. The furniture ⁶ _____ (construct) Josie's husband, from recycled doors and windows. The roof ⁷ _____ (design) to catch rainwater to use inside the house. The house ⁸ _____ (not build) as a home, it ⁹ _____ (create) as an example of eco-friendly housing. Last year it ¹⁰ _____ (visit) over a hundred people.

Total: 9

Past simple passive questions

5 Complete the questions and answers about the text in Exercise 4.

1 When _was_ the eco-house _built_ ?
  In 1995.
2 Who _____ the eco-house _____ ?
  Josie Jackman.
3 Why _____ solar panels _____ ?
  To provide energy for heating.
4 _____ the walls _____ from bricks?
  No, _____ .
5 _____ the roof _____ to catch rainwater?
  Yes, _____ .
6 How many people _____ the house _____ last year?
  Over a hundred.

Total: 5

84 Unit 8 Review

UNIT 8

Language builder

6 Complete the conversation with the missing words. Circle the correct options.

> A: ¹___ my new T-shirt? It ²___ from recycled plastic bottles.
> B: That's amazing! I ³___ a T-shirt like that before.
> A: I ⁴___ it at an eco-shop in town. I ⁵___ it on Green Day next week.
> B: What's Green Day?
> A: It's one day a year when everyone ⁶___ do something green at school.
> B: That's a good idea. If people ⁷___ more to help the environment, we ⁸___ so many problems.
> A: Why don't you come? We ⁹___ great fun.
> B: I'm not sure. If I ¹⁰___ a lot of homework next week, I ¹¹___ to come to your school.
> A: Well, I hope you don't have ¹²___ homework then!

	a	b	c
1	Have you liked	**(b) Do you like**	Were you liking
2	's made	're made	're make
3	didn't see	haven't seen	don't see
4	buy	bought	was buying
5	'll wear	'm going to wear	wear
6	have to	has to	had to
7	were doing	wouldn't do	did
8	don't have	wouldn't have	didn't have
9	always have	have always	always has
10	not have	won't have	don't have
11	might try	won't try	might not try
12	enough	too much	too many

Total: 11

Vocabulary builder

7 Circle the correct options.

1 Most of my T-shirts are made of ___ .
  a rubber   b wood   **c) cotton**
2 Turn off the light to ___ energy.
  a save   b reduce   c consume
3 I only ___ in a test once and I felt awful!
  a screamed   b handed   c cheated
4 My mum doesn't know how to ___ a call on my mobile!
  a do   b make   c get
5 I don't like ___ . It's not nice to talk about other people.
  a arguing   b whispering   c gossiping
6 Ethan's leaving tomorrow but I don't know when he's ___ .
  a picking up   b bringing down   c coming back
7 Sometimes it's nice to have time ___ yourself.
  a by   b on   c of
8 Last week we went to see an orchestra at the concert ___ .
  a theatre   b stage   c hall
9 Before she left, she picked up her expensive red ___ bag.
  a plastic   b leather   c rubber
10 You ___ energy when appliances are on standby.
  a waste   b reduce   c save

Total: 9

Speaking

8 Complete the conversation with the words in the box.

> promise   the thing   meant   happened
> ~~mean~~   never   sorry   completely

> A: Where were you yesterday?
> B: What do you ¹_____**mean**_____ ?
> A: I waited for you at the café for an hour.
> B: Oh no! I'm really ²_____ .
>   I really ³_____ to come, honest!
> A: What ⁴_____ to you?
> B: Well, I ⁵_____ forgot.
> A: I called you but your phone was off.
> B: Yes, I know. ⁶_____ is, I had to stay late at school.
> A: Oh well, ⁷_____ mind. Let's go tomorrow.
> B: Great! I won't be late, I ⁸_____ !

Total: 7

Total: 64

Unit 8 Review   85

Get it right! Unit 8

Present simple passive

Remember that:
We use the present simple form of *be* + the past participle to form the present simple passive
✓ The houses are built from recycled materials.
✗ The houses build from recycled materials.
✗ The houses built from recycled materials.

1 Complete the sentences with the present simple passive form of the verb in brackets.
1 More than 60% of the rubbish in my town ___is recycled___ (recycle).
2 Materials _____ (put) in different rubbish bins.
3 Bottles _____ (collect) in a large bin.
4 Old newspapers _____ (take) to the library for recycling.
5 Old clothes _____ (wash) and taken to special shops to be sold.
6 All of our rubbish _____ (reuse) if possible.

Passive review

2 Circle the correct options to complete the sentences.
1 Someone …
   a said me to go home and get some rest.
   b told me to go home and get some rest.
2 Rachel came in and …
   a asked me to help her clean the kitchen.
   b said me to help her clean the kitchen.
3 I told …
   a to come back tomorrow.
   b them to come back tomorrow.
4 They …
   a said us that they were going to a new school.
   b said that they were going to a new school.
5 We …
   a asked them to give us more time to finish the project.
   b said them to give us more time to finish the project.

the or no article?

Remember that:
- we always use *the* with countries that have **united** or **isles/islands** in their name, e.g. *the UK* and *the USA*. We don't use *the* with other country names.
   ✓ The USA has several renewable energy projects.
   ✗ USA has several renewable energy projects.
- we always use *the* when there is only one of the thing we are talking about, e.g. *the environment*
   ✓ Saving energy is important for the environment.
   ✗ Saving energy is important for environment.
- we don't usually use *the* when we talk about things in a general way.
   ✓ Britain has got lots of sea and wind.
   ✗ Britain has got lots of the sea and wind.

3 Complete the sentences from Unit 8 with *the* or *X* (no article).
1 About a quarter of all the homes in ___X___ South Australia use solar power.
2 Colombia has many renewable sources that can be used to produce _____ energy.
3 In _____ UK it's not sunny very often.
4 Why is the sea so important for _____ planet?
5 _____ solar power isn't big in Britain.
6 _____ government is putting up wind farms.

Spell it right! Past participles

Remember that:
- with irregular verbs, the past simple form of the verb and the past participle are sometimes different.
   ✓ John fell (past simple) off his bike.
   ✓ John has fallen (past participle) off his bike.

4 Write the past simple and past participle form of the verbs from unit 8.

Infinitive	Past simple	Past participle
write	wrote	written
choose		
grow		
throw		
show		

Speaking extra

Reassuring someone

1 ★ ▶ 5.3 Match the sentence halves from the Real talk video in the Student's Book.
1 I had a lot of photos ____
2 I haven't yet but ____
3 I had to talk for two minutes ____
4 My friend and I did ____

a I'm doing one next week.
b about my family and friends.
c a presentation about our summer camp last year.
d so the class loved it (my presentation).

2 ★★ 🔊 25 Listen and answer the questions.

Conversation 1:
1 How long has the girl practised the piano for?
_____

Conversation 2:
2 What has the teacher asked everyone to do?
_____
3 What's the boy's problem?
_____

Conversation 3:
4 What's happening tomorrow?
_____
5 Who can't play?
_____

3 ★ Read the conversation. Why are Lucy and James going shopping?

Lucy:	Oh, you're so lucky you're going to Berlin tomorrow on the school exchange! Are you excited?
James:	Yes, but I'm also a bit worried.
Lucy:	Don't ¹_____ . It'll be fine.
James:	Yes, but what if I don't like my exchange student?
Lucy:	No ²_____ . I'm sure you'll like him.
James:	And what if he doesn't like me?
Lucy:	You'll be ³_____ . You're a really nice person.
James:	And I can't speak German – I don't know what to say.
Lucy:	Of ⁴_____ you can. You're the best in the class.
James:	And I haven't got a present for my exchange student's family.
Lucy:	I think I can ⁵_____ you. Come on, let's go shopping.
James:	Thanks, Lucy. I just can't think of anything to get them.
Lucy:	No problem… it doesn't have to be a big present. It'll ⁶_____ out all right.

4 ★★ 🔊 26 Complete the conversation in Exercise 3 with the words in the box. Then listen and check your answers.

help fine turn worry problem course

Pronunciation focus: Giving instructions

5 ★ 🔊 27 Listen to the instructions. Does the voice go up and then down or down and then up? Listen and repeat.
1 Don't worry!
2 You'll be fine.
3 No problem.
4 You don't need to worry.
5 Of course you can.

6 ★ 🔊 28 Listen to the conversation. Why is Jake very nervous?

7 ★★★ 🔊 28 Listen again and complete the conversation.

Tom:	So are you going to call her or not?
Jake:	Yes… just hold on. I don't know what to say.
Tom:	¹_____ . Just say hello.
Jake:	OK … Hello, Jessica … and then what?
Tom:	²_____ help you. What do you want to say to her?
Jake:	I want to ask her to help me with this project. But I can't do it!
Tom:	³_____ . Just say hello and then ask her to help you.
Jake:	But what if she says no? She might laugh at me.
Tom:	No, she won't. ⁴_____ . Just call her.
Jake:	OK … can't I just send her a text message?
Tom:	No, it's better if you call her. ⁵_____ .
Jake:	I'm really nervous.
Tom:	⁶_____ . She'll help you. I know she will!

8 ★★ 🔊 28 Listen again and check your answers. Then listen and repeat the conversation.

Speaking extra

Expressing surprise

1 ★ ▶ **6.3** Complete the sentences from the Real talk video in the Student's Book with the words in the box.

real music everywhere eyes brother terrified

1 I'm in a room and there are hundreds of spiders and thousands of snakes _____ .
2 When I was little, my _____ locked me in a closet for two hours.
3 I'm terrified of crocodiles but I've never seen a _____ one.
4 I always close my _____ when we take off and I listen to _____ .
5 I don't have any big fears but my dad's _____ of me.

2 ★★ 🔊 **29** Listen and answer the questions.

Conversation 1:
1 What's on the fourth floor?
_____

Conversation 2:
2 Where was the boy yesterday?
_____
3 Who was his best friend?
_____

Conversation 3:
4 What do the girl's parents want to do?
_____
5 What instrument would the girl like to learn?
_____

3 ★ Read the conversation. Where are Oliver and Alice?

Oliver: Where are we going now?
Alice: Well, we've seen the elephants, the lions, and the snakes – ugh! We're going to see the birds next.
Oliver: Birds? No thanks. I'm terrified of birds.
Alice: Are you ¹_____ ?
Oliver: Yeah … well, I just don't like them.
Alice: That's ²_____ . Birds aren't dangerous.
Oliver: Yeah … I know, but …
Alice: I don't ³_____ you! Anyway, the birds are in a zoo – they can't go near you.
Oliver: I don't care. They're too close for me.
Alice: Oh, come on. You're ⁴_____ .
Oliver: Look … it's quite common.
Alice: That can't be ⁵_____ !
Oliver: It is true. People are afraid of dogs, insects, spiders … why not birds?
Alice: What? No ⁶_____ !

4 ★★ 🔊 **30** Complete the conversation in Exercise 3 with the words in the box. Then listen and check.

true serious way believe impossible joking

Pronunciation focus: Sounding surprised

5 ★ 🔊 **31** Listen and repeat the sentences.
1 No way!
2 You're joking.
3 That can't be true.
4 That's impossible.
5 I don't believe you.

6 ★ 🔊 **32** Listen to the conversation. What happened to the unluckiest man in the world's house?

7 ★★★ 🔊 **32** Listen again and complete the conversation.

Lily: Wow! What a story! I'm reading about the unluckiest man in the world.
Simon: Oh, yeah. Why is he so unlucky?
Lily: Well, he fell on a skiing trip in Colorado.
Simon: OK, that's quite common.
Lily: Yes, but there was a snowstorm so the helicopter couldn't take him to the hospital so he had to lie in the snow for four hours.
Simon: ¹_____ ?
Lily: Anyway, they took him to hospital and fixed his leg and sent him home. And then he fell again and broke his other leg!
Simon: What? ²_____ !
Lily: So after that, while he was at home with his two broken legs, a snake came into the house and bit him.
Simon: A snake? ³_____ !
Lily: So they took him to hospital but he got trapped in the lift.
Simon: ⁴_____ !
Lily: Anyway, he got out of the lift, saw the doctor and while he was still in hospital, there was a fire at his house.
Simon: ⁵_____ !
Lily: His house was completely destroyed and he lost everything he had!
Simon: ⁶_____ .
Lily: No, it isn't actually. It's not true at all. But you'd believe anything!

8 ★★ 🔊 **32** Listen again and check your answers. Then listen and repeat the conversation.

Speaking extra

Asking for and giving advice

1 ★ ▶ **7.3** Complete the sentences from the Real talk video in the Student's Book with the words in the box.

| better   advice   helps   problems   wise |

1 When I have _____ with my friends she always says the right thing.
2 He _____ me with everything.
3 She always gives me good _____ .
4 She always makes me feel _____ .
5 She's lived a long time so she's very _____ .

2 ★★ 🔊 **33** Listen and answer the questions.

Conversation 1:
1 What advice does the boy give?
_____

Conversation 2:
2 When's the detention?
_____
3 What's the girl doing this weekend?
_____

Conversation 3:
4 What's in the first message Nathan received?
_____
5 Whose phone number is it?
_____

3 ★ Read the conversation. Did something good or bad happen to Natasha?

John: Hi, Natasha. You look worried. What's the ¹_____ ?
Natasha: Well … I need your ²_____ . A friend of mine posted a horrible photo of me on Facebook and she didn't ask me first.
John: Well, it's always a good ³_____ to ask the person's permission, isn't it?
Natasha: Exactly. And now her friends are making comments about me. What do you think I ⁴_____ do?
John: Well, if I were you, I ⁵_____ reply to any of the comments.
Natasha: Yes, but some of them aren't very nice. My parents say I shouldn't ⁶_____ but they don't understand.
John: Have you ⁷_____ asking your friend to take the photo off Facebook? Maybe we could talk to her ⁸_____ .
Natasha: Thanks, John.

4 ★★ 🔊 **34** Complete the conversation in Exercise 4 with the words in the box. Then listen and check your answers.

| tried   wouldn't   idea   problem |
| worry   advice   together   should |

Pronunciation focus: Sentence stress

5 ★ 🔊 **35** Listen. <u>Underline</u> the stressed words in the sentences. Listen and repeat.
1 I need your advice.
2 If I were you, I'd ask her.
3 Maybe we could go together.
4 Have you tried calling her?
5 It's a good idea to call first.

6 ★ 🔊 **36** Listen to the conversation. How do Emily and Tania decide to help each other?

7 ★★★ 🔊 **36** Listen again and complete the conversation.

Emily: Tania, ¹_____ .
Tania: ²_____ , Emily?
Emily: It's my Maths grade. It's awful. I have to get better grades. What do you think ³_____ ?
Tania: Well, first of all ⁴_____ organise your notes. You should write things down and look at them at home.
Emily: Yes, but I don't understand anything in class.
Tania: ⁵_____ talking to the teacher?
Emily: Mr Banks? Yes, he tries to help me but …
Tania: I'm the same in Music. You've heard me on the piano. I'm terrible. I've talked to my parents but they're so happy with my marks in Maths …
Emily: Oh, but Music is so easy. ⁶_____ spend more time on your Music and less time on Maths. So what did your parents say?
Tania: They said ⁷_____ but I really want to be able to play the piano better.
Emily: Hey! I've got an idea. ⁸_____ work together. You help me with Maths and I'll help you with the piano.
Tania: That's a fantastic idea. Let's start now. Listen to this …

8 ★★ 🔊 **36** Listen again and check your answers. Then listen and repeat the conversation.

Speaking extra

Apologising and explaining

1 ★ ▶ `8.3` **Complete the sentences from the Real talk video in the Student's Book with the verbs in the box.**

> animals   litter   watering plants
> community centre   babysit

1 My friend reads to older people at the _____ once a month.
2 I'm not sure but I know you can help older people with their _____ .
3 You can pick up _____ in the park with the Scouts.
4 I _____ for my little brother all the time and I don't get money for it.
5 You can help in the garden doing things like _____ .

2 ★★ 🔊 `37` **Listen and answer the questions.**

Conversation 1:
1 What does the teacher want?
_____

Conversation 2:
2 What was on at the gallery?
_____
3 Why didn't the girl go?
_____

Conversation 3:
4 What was Joe fixing?
_____
5 How long did Joe wait for Ben?
_____

3 ★ **Read the conversation. Where did Olivia go yesterday? Why didn't Ruby come?**

Olivia:	Hi Ruby. What happened to you yesterday?
Ruby:	Oh, I'm ¹_____ sorry. You went to the park with Scouts to pick up litter, didn't you?
Olivia:	Yes, and you didn't come. What happened?
Ruby:	Yeah, I'm ²_____ . I really ³_____ to come, honest!
Olivia:	Did you fall asleep?
Ruby:	No, the ⁴_____ is, my mum's painting my room and I had to tidy it first.
Olivia:	But why didn't you send me a message?
Ruby:	I completely ⁵_____ . I started tidying … and the ⁶_____ was I just didn't see the time.
Olivia:	Oh well, never ⁷_____ . We're going again next week.
Ruby:	Oh, great. I'll come next week, I ⁸_____ .

4 ★★ 🔊 `38` **Complete the conversation in Exercise 3 with the words in the box. Then listen and check.**

> forgot   really   mind   sorry   thing
> meant   promise   problem

Pronunciation focus: Apologising

5 ★ 🔊 `39` **Listen to the apologies. Does the voice go up or down? Listen and repeat.**
1 I'm sorry.
2 I'm really sorry.
3 I meant to come.
4 I completely forgot.
5 I'll come next time, I promise.

6 ★ 🔊 `40` **Listen to the conversation. What did David want Julia to help him with yesterday?**

7 ★★★ 🔊 `40` **Listen again and complete the conversation.**

David:	Oh, hi Julia. Where were you yesterday? I had to do my French homework. I asked you to come and help me.
Julia:	¹_____ , David. Have you finished it?
David:	Yes, and I've given it to the teacher.
Julia:	²_____ , honest. I know it was really important.
David:	Yes, it was.
Julia:	³_____ . I wanted to do it with you. ⁴_____ , I had to help my dad in the garden.
David:	I sent you text message. Why didn't you answer it?
Julia:	I saw it but ⁵_____ , right at that moment my dad was cutting down a tree and then ⁶_____ .
David:	⁷_____ . So will you help me with my next French homework?
Julia:	More French homework? Well, the thing is … I'm really sorry, but …
David:	What now?
Julia:	Of course, I'll help you, David … tomorrow. ⁸_____
David:	Tomorrow? But I have to do it now! Oh come on, Julia …

8 ★★ 🔊 `40` **Listen again and check your answers. Then listen and repeat the conversation.**

This page is intentionally left blank

Language focus extra

will, might, may + adverbs of possibility

1 Complete the mini-conversations with *will/won't* or *might/might not* and the verb phrases in the box.

> be   play for the team   call me   understand
> pass easily   love it   find the way

1 **A:** I'm worried about the exam.
  B: Don't worry! You*'ll pass easily*.
2 **A:** I hope Sally doesn't get lost.
  B: It's okay. She _____ because she's got a map.
3 **A:** I've bought Luke and Harry a birthday present.
  B: I'm sure they _____ .
4 **A:** David didn't score any goals in the match yesterday.
  B: I know. He _____ next year.
5 **A:** I'm nervous about telling Dad I broke his MP3 player.
  B: Don't worry! He _____ it was an accident.
6 **A:** What instrument is that busker playing?
  B: I don't know. I think it _____ a clarinet.
7 **A:** Is Kate coming to the cinema tonight?
  B: She doesn't know. She's very busy. She _____ later.

2 Complete the mini-conversations with *will/won't* or *might/might not* and the ideas in brackets.

1 **A:** What are you doing this weekend?
  B: I'm not sure. *I might go skateboarding* . (go skateboarding)
2 **A:** Where are you going to meet Megan?
  B: We haven't decided. We _____ . (at the train station)
3 **A:** When is Paula going to see Eric?
  B: I think she _____ . (on Thursday)
4 **A:** Are you coming to the football match tonight?
  B: I can't, but I _____ . (watch it on TV)
5 **A:** Are you going to email me tonight?
  B: Yes, and I _____ (tell) you all the gossip about school!
6 **A:** Can your mum cut my hair this weekend?
  B: She's working, so she _____ . (not have time)
7 **A:** Can I go to your house tonight?'
  B: No, I've got a piano lesson so I _____ . (be at home)

UNIT 5

3 Circle the correct options.
1 I'll **probably** / certainly buy the red one, but I'm going to think about it.
2 She'll **definitely** / **probably** be late. She always is!
3 We **definitely will** / **'ll definitely** do it.
4 They **will probably** / **certainly will** need help.
5 He **probably** / **definitely** won't know, but ask!
6 Computers **will certainly** / **definitely will** take over the world – the question is when!

First conditional + *may/might, be able to*

4 Write sentences in the first conditional.
1 I / angry / criticise / If / might / him, / he / be
  If I criticise him, he might be angry.
2 won't / I / lend / me / her / She / probably / if / ask / her book
  _____
3 my blog / you / might / put it on / If / me / the photo, / send / I
  _____
4 won't / do / that / have / you / any friends / You / if
  _____
5 embarrassed / her / ask / be / you / She / might / if
  _____
6 you / be able to / go home / If / now / you'll / your homework / do
  _____

5 Complete the sentences with the correct form of the verb phrases in the box.

> not listen carefully   not speak loudly   hold his hand
> tell him to call you   go to the park
> send you a friend request   not remind them

1 If it's sunny tomorrow, we'll *go to the park* .
2 If we see him, we _____ .
3 You won't understand if you _____ .
4 He might not be frightened if you _____ .
5 If I go on Facebook, I might _____ .
6 They won't do it if you _____ .
7 I may not be able to hear, if you _____ .

100   Language Focus Extra

Language focus extra

be going to / will / Present continuous

1 Match the sentence halves.
1 I'm going to look up _g_
2 She won't tell her parents what happened ____
3 Jessica and Bea are starting dance classes tomorrow, ____
4 Where are Harry and Eva going to go ____
5 I'm not going to pay for a new one because ____
6 Noah probably won't join the swimming team ____
7 We're going to write an email to the school, ____
8 I'm playing football with Jacob tomorrow ____

a are you interested?
b I hope they answer.
c it was broken when you gave it to me.
d because they might be angry.
e as he's afraid of water.
f against a team from another school.
g some of these new words in a dictionary.
h on holiday this year?

2 Complete the sentences and questions. Use the verb phrases in the box.

> won't be   won't come   're catching
> 'm not going to do   'm looking after
> 's going to rain   are you going   Is she travelling
> ~~'s getting~~   're not going   'll be able to spend

1 My cousin _'s getting_ married in June. I'm really excited!
2 They _____ the 8.20 am train, so we _____ all day together.
3 I _____ much this weekend. I'm very tired.
4 We _____ camping this weekend. It _____ for two days.
5 I _____ my little brother this afternoon. I _____ bored!
6 How long _____ on holiday for, Mia?
7 Tom probably _____ to school tomorrow. He's got a hospital appointment.
8 _____ by plane or by train?

Quantifiers

3 Circle the correct options.
1 We haven't got **much** / **many** time. Be quick or we'll be late!
2 Have we got **a few** / **enough** money to get some water?
3 There are **too many** / **any** options. I can't decide which I prefer.
4 They've got **a little** / **a few** nice T-shirts in your size. What about this one?
5 **A lot of** / **Any** people say that it's a nice place, but I haven't been there yet.
6 I think he was angry because I told him I didn't want **any** / **some** help.
7 **How much** / **How many** is it to go on the roller coaster? Is it expensive?
8 They had a pizza because they didn't have **enough** / **a little** time to cook.

4 Complete the sentences with the words in the box.

> enough   How much   few   too many
> too much   ~~some~~   little   lot

1 You took ___some___ good photos yesterday. Will you send them to me?
2 I had _____ coffee and now I can't sleep.
3 I've got a _____ things to do today. I won't be able to see you.
4 There were _____ people at the concert. I was a bit scared.
5 We've got a _____ orange juice or we've got some water.
6 I don't think we've got _____ money to buy three tickets.
7 _____ pocket money do your parents give you?
8 I have to study a _____ this evening. The exam is tomorrow.

Language focus extra

Second conditional

1 Match the sentence halves.
1. If he went to India,
2. It'd be a great idea
3. There would be less pollution
4. If I was a teacher,
5. You wouldn't believe me
6. If he joined the football team,

a if people didn't use their cars every day.
b he'd make lots of friends.
c if we had enough money.
d if I told you.
e he'd visit the Taj Mahal.
f I wouldn't give any homework.

2 Complete the second conditional sentences. Use the correct form of the verbs in brackets.
1. If I ____had____ (have) enough time, I 'd learn (learn) to play the guitar.
2. She _____ (not be) late for school if she _____ (get up) earlier.
3. If they _____ (know) the answer, they _____ (tell) you.
4. Mr Jones _____ (help) you if you _____ (ask) him nicely.
5. If I _____ (meet) Will Smith, I _____ (ask) for his autograph.
6. Our English _____ (get) better if we _____ (move) to New York.

3 Complete the sentences using the second conditional.
1. Mark doesn't study. He gets bad marks.
   Mark _would get better marks if he studied_.
2. Ana likes swimming. She goes to the pool every day.
   If _____.
3. I'm not going to his house. I don't have time.
   If _____.
4. You don't wear your glasses to read. Your eyes hurt.
   Your _____.
5. We live in the city. We don't have a horse.
   If _____.
6. They aren't on Twitter. I don't follow them.
   I _____.

4 Complete the sentences so they are true for you.
1. If I liked you, I would … _buy you a present_
2. My bedroom would look nice if … _____.
3. If I had a problem, I would … _____.
4. I would get good marks if … _____.
5. If I grew my hair long, … _____.

Second conditional questions

5 Complete the questions with the correct form of the verbs in the box.

| take go say can ~~have~~ need |

1. If you ____had____ a dog, what would you call it?
2. If you didn't feel ill, where _____ you _____ today?
3. What time would we arrive if we _____ the earlier train?
4. If you _____ be a character from a film, who would you be?
5. If he asked you to go out, _____ you _____ yes?
6. Who would you ask if you _____ to borrow some money?

6 Write second conditional questions with the prompts.
1. we / share a bedroom / how often / we / argue?
   If we shared a bedroom, how often would we argue?
2. they / like / it / I / stop / speaking to them?
   _____
3. What / his parents / say / they / know?
   _____
4. you / can / have a super power / what / it / be?
   _____
5. you / live in London / the weather / be / better?
   _____
6. you / be / me / what / you / do?
   _____

Language focus extra

Present simple passive

1 Rewrite the sentences using the present simple passive.
1. They clean the windows every month.
   The _windows are cleaned every month_ .
2. They don't update their blog every day.
   The _____ .
3. People take a lot of photos on mobile phones.
   A _____ .
4. The hotel serves breakfast from 7–10 am.
   Breakfast _____ .
5. They give students a certificate at the end of the year.
   Students _____ .
6. People ask a lot of questions in my class.
   A _____ .

2 Use a word from each box to complete the sentences. Use the present simple passive.

| bananas spaghetti cakes ~~tea~~ fish chocolate |

| ~~drink~~ catch cook bake make grow |

1. _Tea is drunk_ in most countries.
2. _____ from cocoa beans.
3. _____ in an oven.
4. _____ in rivers and at sea.
5. _____ in the Canary Islands.
6. _____ in boiling water.

Past simple passive

3 Complete the text with the past simple passive form of the verbs in brackets.

Modern text messages, or SMS, [1] _were invented_ (invent) in 1992. Early messages [2] _____ (not write) on a mobile phone, they could only be sent from a computer to a phone. The first message in the UK said 'Merry Christmas'. In 1993, the first mobile-to-mobile SMS service [3] _____ (introduce) in Sweden. It wasn't popular immediately, but by 2011, an average of 17.9 billion texts [4] _____ (send) every day. However, technology always moves forward, and in the same year, SMS messages [5] _____ (replace) as the most popular way of sending texts. Chat apps, such as WhatsApp, [6] _____ (use) to send 19 billion texts a day. Experts think this number is going to double in the next two years!

4 Complete the sentences using the past simple passive and *by*.
1. The Wright brothers built the first plane.
   The first plane _was built by the Wright brothers_ .
2. Alfred Nobel invented dynamite.
   Dynamite _____ .
3. Jack Dorsey started Twitter in 2006.
   Twitter _____ .
4. A school teacher wrote the song Happy Birthday.
   The song Happy Birthday _____ .
5. Walt Disney and Ub Iwerks created Mickey Mouse.
   Mickey Mouse _____ .
6. Leonardo da Vinci painted the Mona Lisa.
   The Mona Lisa _____ .

Past simple passive questions

5 Write past simple passive questions with the prompts.
1. In which language / the first book / print?
   In which language was the first book printed?
2. How many hot dogs / eat / by Joey Chestnut in ten minutes?
   _____
3. When / basketball / invent?
   _____
4. Which language / the English word yoghurt / take / from?
   _____
5. How many people / the 2014 World Cup final / watch / by?
   _____
6. In what year / the first computer game / release?
   _____

6 Match the answers (a–f) with the questions in Exercise 5.
a 69   Question: ___
b 1976   Question: ___
c 1 billion   Question: ___
d Turkish   Question: ___
e German   Question: _1_
f 1891   Question: ___

Irregular verbs

infinitive	past simple	past participle
be	was/were	been
become	became	become
begin	began	begun
break	broke	broken
build	built	built
buy	bought	bought
catch	caught	caught
choose	chose	chosen
come	came	come
do	did	done
drink	drank	drunk
drive	drove	driven
eat	ate	eaten
fall	fell	fallen
feed	fed	fed
feel	felt	felt
find	found	found
fly	flew	flown
get	got	got
give	gave	given
go	went	gone
have	had	had
hear	heard	heard
keep	kept	kept
know	knew	known
learn	learnt/learned	learnt/learned
leave	left	left
lose	lost	lost
make	made	made
meet	met	met
pay	paid	paid
put	put	put
read	read	read
run	ran	run
say	said	said
see	saw	seen
send	sent	sent
sit	sat	sat
sleep	slept	slept
speak	spoke	spoken
spend	spent	spent
swim	swam	swum
take	took	taken
teach	taught	taught
tell	told	told
think	thought	thought
wear	wore	worn
win	won	won
write	wrote	written

Phonemic symbols

consonants

/p/	pencil
/b/	bag
/t/	town
/d/	day
/tʃ/	cheese
/dʒ/	juice
/k/	cake
/g/	get
/f/	food
/v/	very
/θ/	Thursday
/ð/	that
/s/	speak
/z/	zebra
/ʃ/	shoe
/ʒ/	usually
/m/	mum
/n/	name
/ŋ/	sing
/h/	house
/l/	like
/r/	red
/w/	water
/j/	you

vowels

/i:/	see
/ɪ/	sit
/ʊ/	book
/u:/	zoo
/e/	pen
/ə/	teacher
/ɜ:/	bird
/ɔ:/	boring
/æ/	that
/ʌ/	run
/ɑ:/	car
/ɒ/	lost

diphthongs

/eɪ/	say
/ɪə/	hear
/ʊə/	pure
/ɔɪ/	enjoy
/əʊ/	know
/eə/	chair
/aɪ/	buy
/aʊ/	now

Thanks and acknowledgments

The authors and publishers would like to thank a number of people whose support has proved invaluable during the planning, writing and production process of this course.

We would like to thank Diane Nicholls for researching and writing the Get it Right pages, Alice Martin for writing the original Starter Unit, Ingrid Wisniewska for writing the original Review sections and Mick Green for writing the original Grammar Extra sections.

The authors and publishers are grateful to the following contributors:
Blooberry: concept design
emc design Limited: text design and layout
emc design Limited: cover design
David Morritt and Ian Harker – DSound: audio recordings
Ruth Cox: editing

Development of this publication has made use of the Cambridge English Corpus (CEC). The CEC is a computer database of contemporary spoken and written English, which currently stands at over one billion words. It includes British English, American English and other varieties of English. It also includes the Cambridge Learner Corpus, developed in collaboration with the University of Cambridge ESOL Examinations. Cambridge University Press has built up the CEC to provide evidence about language use that helps to produce better language teaching materials.

The authors and publishers acknowledge the following sources of copyright material and are grateful for the permissions granted. While every effort has been made, it has not always been possible to identify the sources of all the material used, or to trace all copyright holders. If any omissions are brought to our notice, we will be happy to include the appropriate acknowledgements on reprinting.

p. 5 (BL): Corbis/Clifford White; p. 6 (B): Alamy/©Picture Partners; p. 8 (TR): age fotostock/stefano gulmanelli; p. 9 (TR): Getty Images/David Trood; p. 10 (CL): Alamy/©Patrick Eden; p. 11 (BL): Shutterstock Images/Benjamin Simeneta; p. 12 (C): Shutterstock Images/A.Hornung; p. 12 (B): Alamy/©PhotoAlto; p. 15 (BR): Alamy/©MBI; p. 17 (CR): Getty Images/Claudia Dewald; p. 20 (C): Shutterstock Images/Anchiy; p. 21 (BL): Alamy/©Terry Foster; p. 21 (C): Alamy/©My Lit'l Eye; p. 22 (BL): Shutterstock Images/Alexander Raths; p. 25 (TR): Shutterstock Images/lzf; p. 28 (BR): REX/Nils Jorgensen; p. 29 (CR): Alamy/©Roberto Herrett; p. 30 (BR): Alamy/©Scott Hortop Images; p. 31 (BL): Alamy/©Marek Stepan; p. 32 (B): Corbis/Paul Hackett; p. 37 (BR): Alamy/©Cate Brown; p. 38 (TR): Alamy/©Art Directors & TRIP; p. 39 (TL): Shutterstock Images/Monkey Business Images; p. 39 (BR): Shutterstock Images/Mitotico; p. 40 (TL): Shutterstock Images/Roland Zihlmann; p. 41 (TC): Shutterstock Images/ilovezion; p. 41 (TR): Shutterstock Images/Ammit Jack; p. 41 (BL): Shutterstock Images/Anton_Ivanov; p. 42 (CL): Shutterstock Images/NAN728; p. 42 (BL): Getty Images/Rolf Bruderer; p. 47 (TR): Getty Images/Zero Creatives; p. 48 (CL): Shutterstock Images/ARENA Creative; p. 49 (TL): Alamy/©Design Pics Inc.; p. 49 (BR): Getty Images/monkeybusinessimages; p. 50 (BL): Alamy/©Picture Partners; p. 51 (TL): Shutterstock Images/Monkey Business Images; p. 52 (TR): Shutterstock Images/MJTH; p. 54 (CL): Shutterstock Images/wallybird; p. 58 (CR): Alamy/©Westend61 GmbH; p. 60 (TR): Shutterstock Images/Refat; p. 61 (BL): Alamy/©Angela Hampton Picture Library; p. 62 (B): Alamy/©Emiliano Joanes; p. 68 (CL): Alamy/©Jenny Matthews; p. 69 (TL): Shutterstock Images/Olimpik; p. 69 (BR): Shutterstock Images/Photographee.eu; p. 71 (BL): Shutterstock Images/Monkey Business Images; p. 72 (C): Alamy/©imageBROKER; p. 74 (TL): Shutterstock Images/sonya etchison; p. 78 (BL): Alamy/©Jim West; p. 78 (TR): Shutterstock Images/Bakalusha; p. 80 (TR): Alamy/©Islandstock; p. 81 (TL): Shutterstock Images/bikeriderlondon; p. 81 (BL): Alamy/©Michael Klinec; p. 82 (BL): Getty Images/Jupiterimages; p. 84 (TR): Alamy/©Andrew Butterton; p. 88 (B): Alamy/©Caroline Commins; p. 89 (BL): Shutterstock Images/Nagy-Bagoly Arpad; p. 90 (CR): Shutterstock Images/Prudkov; p. 91 (CR): Alamy/©Keith Pritchard/ARGO Images.

Front cover photograph by Getty Images/Eduardo Garcia.

The publishers are grateful to the following illustrators:

David Belmonte p. 19, 27; Russ Cook p. 3 (TL), 35, 65, 75; Nigel Dobbyn p. 14, 57, 77; Mark Draisey p. 7, 59, 68, 70; Mark Duffin p. 9, 29, 79; Andrew Painter p. 18; Martin Sanders p. 3 (R), 55; Tony Wilkins p. 20, 47.

All video stills by kind permission of Discovery Communications, LLC 2015.

CAMBRIDGE
UNIVERSITY PRESS

University Printing House, Cambridge CB2 8BS, United Kingdom

One Liberty Plaza, 20th Floor, New York, NY 10006, USA

477 Williamstown Road, Port Melbourne, VIC 3207, Australia

314–321, 3rd Floor, Plot 3, Splendor Forum, Jasola District Centre, New Delhi – 110025, India

79 Anson Road, #06–04/06, Singapore 079906

Cambridge University Press is part of the University of Cambridge.

It furthers the University's mission by disseminating knowledge in the pursuit of education, learning and research at the highest international levels of excellence.

www.cambridge.org
Information on this title: www.cambridge.org/9781107489400

© Cambridge University Press 2015

This publication is in copyright. Subject to statutory exception and to the provisions of relevant collective licensing agreements, no reproduction of any part may take place without the written permission of Cambridge University Press.

First published 2015

20 19 18 17 16 15 14 13 12 11 10 9 8

Printed in Malaysia by Vivar Printing

A catalogue record for this publication is available from the British Library

ISBN 978-1-107-46764-4 Student's Book with Online Workbook and Online Practice
ISBN 978-1-107-46762-0 Student's Book
ISBN 978-1-107-46773-6 Workbook with Online Practice
ISBN 978-1-107-48938-7 Combo A with Online Workbook and Online Practice
ISBN 978-1-107-48940-0 Combo B with Online Workbook and Online Practice
ISBN 978-1-107-46775-0 Teacher's Book
ISBN 978-1-107-46776-7 Audio CDs (3)
ISBN 978-1-107-46779-8 Video DVD
ISBN 978-1-107-48942-4 Presentation Plus DVD-ROM

Additional resources for this publication at www.cambridgelms.org/eyesopen

Cambridge University Press has no responsibility for the persistence or accuracy of URLs for external or third-party internet websites referred to in this publication, and does not guarantee that any content on such websites is, or will remain, accurate or appropriate. Information regarding prices, travel timetables, and other factual information given in this work is correct at the time of first printing but Cambridge University Press does not guarantee the accuracy of such information thereafter.

Your notes

Your notes